CUMBRIA-WESTMO..... ..

FEDERATION OF WOMEN'S INSTITUTES

Treats for Tea Time

Dedicated to past WI members who have set the standard for our current generation of cooks and to inspire the future generation to follow in their footsteps

Published by Helm Press on behalf of
Cumbria-Westmorland Federation of Women's Institutes,
W.I. Headquarters, The Masonic Hall, Station Road, Kendal.
Cumbria LA9 6BT

Registered Charity No 240758

First published in 1989

Reprinted and revised in 2002

ISBN 0 9540497 2 1

Typeset and printed by Miller Turner Printers, Kendal
Tel: 01539 740937

Foreword

"These recipes, from members of Cumbria-Westmorland Federation of Women's Institutes are intended for 'treats' for tea-time, but no doubt they will be eaten at other times too."

...so says the original 'Treats for Tea-Time' book. In this reprint, as a result of overwhelming demand from baking devotees at home and abroad, only the weights have been modernised. All other aspects remain purposely unaltered, so that above all else the taste remains the same!

Cumbria-Westmorland Federation expresses its sincere thanks to Anne Bonney of Helm Press for her encouragement, enthusiasm and support in getting this book back into circulation.

Shirley Pelluca

Federation Chairman
September 2002

Contents

OVEN TEMPERATURE CHART

Electricity		Gas	
Fahrenheit	Celsius		
225	110	¼	Very Slow
250	125	½	Very Slow
275	140	1	Slow
300	150	2	Slow
325	165	3	Moderate
350	180	4	Moderate
375	190	5	Moderately Hot
400	200	6	Moderately Hot
425	220	7	Hot
450	230	8	Hot
475	240	9	Very Hot

The above is a guide only. To be absolutely sure refer to your own cooker instruction book.

METRIC MEASURES
Weight

Recommended gram (g) conversion to nearest 25g

1 Imperial ounces – 25 g
2 Imperial ounces – 50 g
3 Imperial ounces – 75 g
4 Imperial ounces – 125 g
5 Imperial ounces – 150 g
6 Imperial ounces – 175 g
7 Imperial ounces – 200 g
8 Imperial ounces – 225 g

9 Imperial ounces – 250 g
10 Imperial ounces – 275 g
11 Imperial ounces – 300 g
12 Imperial ounces – 350 g
13 Imperial ounces – 375 g
14 Imperial ounces – 400 g
15 Imperial ounces – 425 g
16 Imperial ounces – 450 g

Volume

2 fl oz 55 ml
3 fl oz 75 ml
4 fl oz 120 ml
5 fl oz (¼ pt) 150 ml
6 fl oz 170 ml
7 fl oz 200 ml

8 fl oz 230 ml
10 fl oz (½ pt) 275 ml
12 fl oz 340 ml
15 fl oz (¾ pt) 425 ml
20 fl oz (1 pt) 570 ml
25 fl ox (1¼ pt) 725 ml

Always follow either the metric measures or the imperial ones. It is not wise to change from one to the other in a recipe.

Scones

All-in-one Fruit Scones
Brown Farmhouse Scones
Butterscotch Scones
Cheese Scones
Cherry Lemon Scones
Drop Scones
Fat Rascals
Ginger Scones
Orange & Raisin Drop Scones
Pumpkin Scones
Scones — Scottish Recipe
Syrup Oat Scones
Treacle Scones

ALL-IN-ONE FRUIT SCONES

2 oz. soft margarine (50 g)	2 oz. sultanas (50 g)
8 oz. S.R. flour (225 g)	1 oz. caster sugar (25 g)
1 level teasp, baking powder	7 tblsp. fresh or sour milk

Sieve flour and baking powder. Add all other ingredients. Mix with a wooden spoon to form dough. Knead lightly on board until smooth. Roll out and cut out. Brush with milk. Bake 425°F/ 220°C for 12-15 minutes.

Crosscrake W.I.

BROWN FARMHOUSE SCONES

2 oz. flour (50 g)	6 oz. wholemeal flour (175 g)
½ level teasp. salt	3 level teasp. baking powder
1½ teasp. caster sugar	4 tblsp. milk
2 oz. butter or margarine (50 g)	

Sieve the flour, salt and sugar, rub in fat, stir in wholemeal flour and baking powder. Mix all the ingredients well, then add milk (using more if required) to make a soft dough. Knead into a flat round on a lightly floured board. Place the scone on a greased baking sheet and mark into six triangles with the back of a floured knife. Bake in a hot oven (450°F) for about 10 minutes. When nearly cooked, break the triangles apart and finish cooking. Split and serve hot with butter.

Burton W.I.

BUTTERSCOTCH SCONES

7 oz. P. flour (200 g)	Pinch salt
1 oz. cornflour (25 g)	¼ pint milk (approx.) (150 ml)
1 oz. butter (25 g)	Soft butter for spreading
1½ level teasp. baking powder	1½–2 tblsp. soft brown sugar

Sieve flour, cornflour, baking powder & salt into a bowl. Rub in butter and mix with sufficient milk to form a soft dough. Knead and form into an oblong about ¼" thick, spread with butter and then sprinkle on the sugar. Form into a roll and cut into ½" slices. Put on a baking tray, cut side down and bake at 400°F for 10 mins.

The Lakes W.I. Market

CHEESE SCONES

8 oz P. flour (225 g)
2 teasp. baking powder
1 heaped teasp. mustard powder
1 pinch salt

2 oz. grated cheese (50 g)
2 oz. butter (50 g)
1 egg and ½ pint milk
beaten together (275 ml)

Mix dry ingredients together. Rub in butter. Add cheese – saving a little. Gradually add beaten egg and milk – you may not need it all – should form a soft dough. Rest in fridge for 30 mins. Roll out and cut. Top with grated cheese. Bake on top shelf of oven for ten minutes – Gas Mark 6/400°F.

Windermere W.I.

CHERRY LEMON SCONES

1 lb S.R flour (450 g)
Pinch salt
1 teasp. baking powder
Juice and grated lemon rind
4 oz. soft margarine (125 g)

2 oz caster sugar (50 g)
4 oz. glacé cherries (125 g)
2 tblsp. plain yoghurt
milk to mix
1 egg to glaze

Preheat oven to 220°C.
Sift flour, salt and baking powder together. Rub in margarine. Stir in sugar, lemon rind and chopped glacé cherries. Add lemon juice, yoghurt and milk to mix to a soft dough. Roll out on a floured surface to about ¾" thick. Cut into rounds, place on a baking sheet, brush with egg. Bake 10–15 mins.

Kirkby Lonsdale Market W.l.

DROP SCONES

½ lb P. flour (225 g)
Pinch of salt
1 large egg
½ teasp. bicarbonate of soda

¾ teasp. cream of tartar
3 dessp. caster sugar
Milk to mix
1 tblsp. of cream

Sieve all dry ingredients, add beaten egg and cream. Add milk to make a smooth dropping consistency. Drop in tablespoon on to a greased girdle and turn when bubbles appear on the surface. Cool the scones in a tea towel on a wire tray.

Ambleside W.l.

FAT RASCALS

8 oz. S.R. flour (225 g)
4 oz. lard (or lard & marg) (125 g)
3 oz. sugar (75 g)

2 oz. currants (50 g)
1 oz. sultanas (25 g)
Water or beaten egg

Rub fat into flour and add the other ingredients. Mix to a fairly soft, but not sticky dough with a little water or beaten egg. Roll out to ½" thickness and cut into rounds. Bake in hot oven (425°F/220°C) for about 15 minutes until nicely brown.

Casterton W.l.

GINGER SCONES

8 oz. P. flour (225 g)
1 oz. margarine (25 g)
1 oz. caster sugar (25 g)
2 level tblsp. of syrup
1 egg

1 level teasp. cream of tartar
Pinch salt
2 level teasp. ground ginger
1 level teasp. bicarbonate soda

Rub fat into sieved flour. Add all other dry ingredients. Warm syrup and add. Mix into a soft dough. Roll out and cut into rounds, brush over with egg or milk. Bake in a hot oven 10–15 minutes.

Kendal Parr W.I.

ORANGE & RAISIN DROP SCONES

8 oz. S.R. flour (225 g)
3 oz. raisins (75 g)
½ oz. butter, melted (10 g)
1 level teasp. salt
½ level teasp. baking powder

4 level tblsp. caster sugar
Grated rind & juice of 1 orange
2 eggs
½ pint milk (275 ml)

Sift together flour, salt, sugar and baking powder. Add the grated orange rind. Gradually beat in the eggs, milk and melted butter. Stir in 2 tablespoons orange juice and the raisins. Lightly butter and heat a griddle iron or frying pan and drop small rounds from a spoon. Cook for a few minutes until bubbles show on the surface of the scone mixture, then turn over carefully to repeat on the other side. Serve warm or cold on day of making.

Preston Patrick & Preston Richard W.I.

PUMPKIN SCONES

10 oz. P. flour (275 g)
2 oz. butter (50 g)
2 oz. sugar (50 g)
2 level teasp, baking powder

½ cup mashed pumpkin
¼ pint milk (150 ml)
1 egg

Cream butter and sugar, add pumpkin and the egg, well beaten. Slowly add the milk. Add flour, sifted with baking powder and mix well. Knead lightly and roll out to 1½" thick. Cut into small rounds, place on a floured tray and cook for 20 minutes at 400°F. Place on a rack to cool.

Old Hutton W.I.

11

SCOTTISH RECIPE SCONES

6 oz. S.R. flour (175 g) Milk to mix
2½ oz. caster sugar (60 g) 1 small egg
2½ oz. margarine (soft or hard) (60 g)

Rub margarine into flour. Add other ingredients to form a soft dough. Roll out to ¾" thick. Cut into small rounds with a cutter. Place on a floured baking tray or in individual bun tins. Cook in centre of hot oven (Gas Mark 7/425°F) for about ten minutes. Remove from tray and leave to cool. These scones can have dried fruit added to them or cinnamon sprinkled on top with sugar, before cooking.

Windermere W.I.

SYRUP OAT SCONES

12 oz. S.R. flour (350 g) 2 oz. porridge oats (50 g)
3 level teasp. baking powder 4 level teasp. golden syrup
1 level teasp. ground ginger 7 fluid oz. milk (200 ml)
3 oz. butter (75 g) at room temperature

Sift the flour with the baking powder and ground ginger into a large bowl. Rub in the butter until the mixture resembles fine breadcrumbs. Stir in the oats. Warm the syrup and add to the milk. Mix in dry ingredients to soft dough adding more milk if necessary. Roll out to ½" thick on a floured surface and cut with cutters or into triangles. Place the scones on a greased tray in a pre-heated oven at 230°C/450°F. Serve immediately.

Orton W.I.

TREACLE SCONES

½ lb. S.R. Flour (225 g) 2 oz. margarine (50 g)
2 oz. sugar (50 g) 1 egg
½ teasp, mixed spice 2 tblsp. treacle
Pinch salt ½ cup boiling water

Put dry ingredients into a bowl, mix and make a well in middle. Into this put egg, treacle and fat that has been melted in the boiling water. Mix together. Drop dessp. full of mixture onto greased baking sheet, allow for spreading. Cook in moderate oven until springy to the touch. Butter on underside before eating. Best if eaten same day.

Levens W.I.

Tea Breads

Apricot Tea Bread
Arnside Tea Bread
Banana, Cherry and Nut Loaf
Banana Tea Bread
Barm Brack
Boiled Fruit Loaf 1
Boiled Fruit Loaf 2
Bran Fruit Loaf
Bubble Loaf
Cereal Fruit Loaf
Chelsea Buns
Date Loaves
Date and Walnut Loaf
Fig Loaf
Lakeland Tea Loaf
Lemon Bread 1
Lemon Bread 2
Malt Bread
Nut Loaf
Orange & Sultana Loaf
Overnight Tea Bread
Quick Cup Loaf
Spicy Tea Bread
Tropical Tea Bread
Walnut & Orange Tea Bread

APRICOT TEA BREAD

8 oz. S.R. flour (225 g)   2 oz. margarine (50 g)
4 oz. dried apricots (125 g)   4 oz. golden syrup (125 g)
2 oz. chopped almonds (50 g)   1 egg
2 oz. light brown soft sugar (50 g) 5 tblsp. milk

Pour boiling water onto apricots and leave for 1 hour. Drain and cut into small pieces. Put flour into a bowl. Stir in the apricots, nuts and sugar. Melt margarine and syrup together. Add the beaten egg and milk. Mix into the dry ingredients. Pour into a greased lined 2 lb loaf tin. Bake at 350°F for 1 hour.

Storth W.I.

ARNSIDE TEA BREAD

1 oz. yeast (25 g)   3 egg yolks
1 teasp. sugar   ½ teasp. vanilla essence
¼ pint warm water (150 ml)   Grated rind of one lemon
14 oz. strong white flour (400 g) 2 oz. raisins (50 g)
½ teasp. salt   2 oz. sultanas (50 g)
1 oz. caster sugar (25 g)   2 oz. mixed peel (50 g)
4 oz butter or margarine (125 g)

Make as bread dough but do not add fruit until second kneading. Bake in 2 small loaf tins 400°F for 12 mins, reduce to 325°F for further 10–12 minutes. Glaze, if liked, with melted butter while still warm.

Arnside W.I.

BANANA AND CHERRY NUT LOAF

2 bananas   4 oz. soft margarine (125 g)
2 oz. cherries (50 g)   8 oz. S.R. flour (225 g)
2 oz. nuts (50 g)   2 eggs beaten
6 oz. light brown sugar (175 g)

Sieve flour and pinch of salt together, add margarine, sugar, chopped cherries and nuts and beaten eggs. Peel and mash bananas with fork and add to mixture. Beat well together. Bake in 2 lb loaf tin in moderate oven for 1¼-1½ hours. Allow to cool before removing from tin. Cut and butter.

Levens W.I.

BANANA TEA BREAD

7 oz. S.R. flour (200 g)   6 oz. sugar (175 g)
¼ level teasp. bicarbonate soda   2 eggs (beaten)
½ level teasp. salt   1 lb. bananas (mashed) (450 g)
3 oz. butter (75 g)   4 oz. nuts (chopped roughly) (125 g)

Grease and line oblong cake tin – 2 lb size. Sift the flour, soda and salt. Cream the butter and sugar until pale and fluffy and add the egg, a little at a time, beating well after each addition. Add the bananas and beat again. Stir the flour and nuts in. Put into a tin and bake in the centre of the oven (350°F/Gas Mark 4) for 1¼ hours until well risen and just firm. Turn out and cool on a cooling tray. Best kept 24 hours, before serving sliced, and buttered.

Barbon W.I.

BARM BRACK (TEA LOAF)

12 fl.oz. cold tea (340 ml)   10 oz. S.R. flour (275 g)
7 oz. soft brown sugar (200 g)   1 egg
12 oz. mixed dried fruit (350 g)   ½ teasp. nutmeg or mixed spice
2 oz. glacé cherries (50 g)

Put tea, sugar, dried fruit and cherries in a bowl, cover and leave to soak overnight. Next day, add sifted flour and spice, plus the beaten egg, to make a smooth mixture. Turn into a well greased 8" round cake tin or 2 lb loaf tin and cook for about 1¾ hours, Gas Mark 4/350°F, centre shelf. Serve sliced with butter. Freezes well.

Kendal Parr W.I.

BOILED FRUIT LOAF (I)

1 cup sugar   4 oz. margarine (125 g)
1 cup mixed fruit   1 cup milk

Put into pan and bring to boil. Boil gently for three minutes. Allow to cool. Then add, 2 cups S.R. flour and 1 beaten egg. Place mixture into lined loaf tin and bake for approx one hour in a moderately hot oven (350°F). Serve sliced and buttered.

Milnthorpe W.I. Market

BOILED FRUIT LOAF (2)

8 oz. margarine (225 g)
2 cups sugar
4 cups dried fruit
2 cups water

2 teasp. bicarbonate of soda
1 lb S.R. flour (450 g)
4 eggs

In large pan mix margarine, sugar, fruit, water and bicarbonate of soda. Bring to boil, simmer for 5 mins, cool for 5 mins. Pour over S.R. flour. Mix in 4 beaten eggs. Bake at 325°-350°F for 1 hour or little longer. Makes 2-2 lb loaves. Serve buttered.

Witherslack W.I.

BRAN FRUIT LOAF

1 cup All Bran
1 cup soft brown sugar
1 cup S.R. flour

1 cup milk
1 cup sultanas and currants (mixed)

Put all ingredients in a bowl and mix well. Allow to soak for 1 hour. Bake in a loaf tin for 1 hour at 200°C. Slice and butter when cold.

Sedbergh W.I. Market

BUBBLE LOAF

8 oz. strong white flour
  or P. flour (225 g)
1 level teasp. caster sugar
2 oz. melted butter (50 g)
1 beaten egg
½ teasp. caster sugar
1 teasp. salt

½ oz. fresh yeast (10 g)
  or 1 level tblsp. dried yeast
1 oz lard (25 g)
4 fluid oz. milk (120 ml)
3 oz. caster sugar (75 g)
  and 1 teasp. cinnamon

1 oz. each of walnuts, glacé cherries, crystallised ginger (chopped) (25 g)

Rub fresh yeast into one third of the flour, add warm milk and ½ teaspoon sugar. Mix to a batter and leave in a warm place until frothy – about 10 minutes. Sieve rest of flour and salt, rub in lard, add yeast mixture and beaten egg to dry ingredients. Knead until smooth, 2 to 3 mins. Leave to rise in a warm place until doubled in size – about 1 hour. Knock back and shape into 24 walnut- sized pieces. In one bowl, place melted butter, in another the mixed sugar and cinnamon. Dip each piece first into the butter, then the sugar and cinnamon. Lay half the pieces around an 8" tube tin, sprinkle with half the nuts, ginger and cherries. Layer the rest on top with the remainder of the nut mixture. Cover with greased polythene and put in a warm place for about 45 mins. This can also be done using a 2 lb loaf tin. Cook in a fairly hot oven 200°C/ 400°F/Gas Mark 6 for 15 – 20 mins. Cool for 5 mins. Turn out carefully.

Hawkshead & Outgate W.I.

CEREAL FRUIT LOAF

2 oz. Weetabix, crumbled (50 g) or whole wheat cereal
8 oz. soft brown sugar (225 g)
6 oz. mixed dried fruit (175 g)
7 oz. S.R. flour (200 g)
1 oz. finely chopped walnuts (25 g)
½ pint milk (275 ml)
1 egg
¼ teasp salt

Soak Weetabix, sugar and dried fruits in milk for 12 hours. Add the egg, flour and walnuts. Mix together, turn into a greased loaf tin and bake at 325oF for 1–1½ hrs.

Rusland W.I.

CHELSEA BUNS

4 oz. Butter (100 g)
¼ pt milk (150 ml)
4 oz castor sugar (100 g)
½ oz fresh yeast (15 g)
2 eggs
1 lb strong white flour (450 g)
A little lard
3 oz currants (75 g)

Melt the butter, add most of the milk and 3 oz (75 g) sugar and warm together. Cream the yeast with the rest of the milk; beat the eggs. Sieve the flour, add the warmed ingrediants and the creamed yeast to the flour, together with the beaten eggs and mix thoroughly. Cover with a clean, damp cloth and put to rise in a warm place until the dough has doubled in size. Roll dough to an oblong, brush with fat, add fruit and sugar, and roll up into a sausage shape. Cut slices 1″ (2.5 cm) thick and place close together in a greased straight-sided tin. Allow to rise for 25 minutes. Bake in hot oven 450–230°C, Gas Mark 8 for 15–20 minutes until well risen and golden. While still warm brush with a sugar glaze.

Ambleside W.I.

DATE LOAVES IN 9 EASY STEPS

Put into mixing bowl
1. ½ lb cooking dates (chopped small) (225 g)
2. Add 1 teasp. bicarbonate of soda
3. Pour over 1 cup boiling water, leave to stand for 1 hour
4. Add 1 cup sugar
5. 1 tblsp. soft margarine
6. 1 egg
7. 2 cups S.R. flour and stir well
8. Put mixture into 2 greased 1 lb loaf tins
9. Bake at Gas Mark 3/325°F/170°C for 1½ hours

These loaves keep very well and are better if kept for 1 week before eating.

Barbon W.I.

DATE AND WALNUT LOAF

1 cup hot water	1 beaten egg
1 teasp. bicarbonate of soda	1½ cups P. flour
1 cup chopped dates	1 cup walnuts
1 cup sugar	pinch of salt
1 tblsp. margarine	

Put chopped dates with hot water and bicarbonate into soak until cooled. Cream sugar and margarine, add beaten egg. Pour into dates. Add flour, salt and walnuts. Bake in loaf tin for approximately 1 hour at 325°F. Slice and butter when cold.

Broughton Mills and Woodland W.I.

FIG LOAF

4 oz. All Bran (125 g)	½ pint milk (275 ml)
4 oz. brown sugar (125 g)	4 oz. S.R. flour (125 g)
2 tblsp. black treacle	½ teasp. ground ginger
4 oz. dried figs – chopped (125 g)	

Soak All Bran, sugar, treacle and figs in milk for 30 mins until milk has been absorbed. Mix flour and ginger and stir into fruit mixture. Turn into a greased 2 lb loaf tin. Bake 45/55 minutes (oven 180°C/350°F/Gas Mark 4) until skewer pierced through centre comes out clean.

Cliburn W.I.

LAKELAND TEA LOAF

Into a saucepan put 1 cup cold water, 1 cup raisins or sultanas, 1 cup sugar, 4 oz. (125 g) soft margarine or butter. Bring to the boil and simmer for 10 minutes. Remove from heat and cool. Beat in 1 heaped teasp. bicarbonate of soda, pinch of mixed spice if liked, 1 medium egg lightly beaten and 2 cups self-raising flour. Pour mixture into a 2 lb loaf tin and bake for 1 hour and 10 minutes at 160°C/325°F. Use standard tea-cup holding 8 fl. oz (230 ml). Serve sliced and buttered.

Preston Patrick & Preston Richard W.I.

LEMON BREAD (1)

8 oz. caster sugar (225 g)   Grated rind of one lemon
3 oz. margarine (75 g)   and one orange
1 large egg   ¼ pint milk (150 ml)
8 oz. P. flour (225 g)   1 level teasp. baking powder

For the topping: The juice of one lemon and 1 tablespoon caster sugar. Beat caster sugar and margarine. Beat in lemon and orange rind with the egg, then sift in the flour and baking powder, mix all together with the milk. Bake in a 2 lb loaf tin at 325oF, for 1¼ hours. Put topping on when cool.

Preston Patrick & Preston Richard W.I.

LEMON BREAD (2)

3 oz. margarine (75 g)   6 oz. S.R. flour (175 g)
6 oz. caster sugar (175 g)   ½ teasp. salt
2 eggs   Grated rind of 1 lemon
½ cup milk

TOPPING
3 oz. caster sugar (75 g)   Juice of 1 lemon

Cream together margarine and sugar, add beaten eggs, milk and lemon rind. Fold in flour. Put mixture into 2 lb loaf tin and bake for 15 minutes at Gas Mark 4/350°F/180°C and then 45 minutes at Gas Mark 3/325°F/170°C. While cake is baking, mix together the lemon juice and caster sugar for topping. As soon as the cake is out of the oven, and whilst it is still in the tin, pour over the topping and leave to harden as the cake cools.

Barbon W.I.

MALT BREAD

8 oz. S.R. flour (225 g)   1 teasp. salt
4 oz. sultanas (125 g)   ½ teasp. bicarbonate of soda
¼ pint milk (150 ml)   2 tblsp. syrup
1 heaped dessp. brown sugar   2 tblsp. malt extract

Mix flour, salt and bicarbonate of soda together. Add sugar and sultanas. Melt syrup and malt extract together. Add the milk and pour onto dry ingredients. Mix well and pour into a 2 lb loaf tin. Bake in oven 325°F-350°F, for approx, 1 hr.

Torver W.I.

NUT LOAF

2 cups S.R. flour
1 cup sugar
1 cup sultanas or mixed fruit

1 cup chopped walnuts
Pinch salt
1 cup of milk to mix

Mix dry ingredients, add milk and stir to a soft mixture. Divide between two 1 lb loaf tins greased or lined with paper. Bake in the middle of oven for 40 mins at 190°C. Serve buttered.

Bowness-on-Windermere W.I.

ORANGE & SULTANA LOAF

12 oz. S.R flour (350 g)
2 oz. caster sugar (50 g)
4 oz. sultanas (125 g)
4 oz. butter (125 g)

4 tblsp. orange marmalade
2 eggs
¼ pint milk (150 ml)
Pinch of salt

Mix together all dry ingredients. Warm the marmalade and add the butter. When the butter melts add to the dry ingredients with the eggs and milk. Mix well and put into 2 lb loaf tin and cook at 325°F for 1 hour 10 minutes approximately.

Bouth W.I.

OVERNIGHT TEA BREAD

12 tblsp strong tea
1 lb mixed dried fruit (450 g)
6 oz. soft brown sugar (175 g)
1 egg (slightly beaten)

1 oz. soft margarine (melted) (25 g)
9 oz. P. flour (250 g) – sieved with
½ teasp. bicarbonate of soda

Place tea, mixed dried fruit and sugar in a bowl, cover and leave overnight. Stir in egg and melted margarine. Fold in sieved ingredients. Place mixture in greased and lined 2 lb loaf tin, smooth top. Bake in moderate oven Gas Mark 4/350°F/180°C on middle shelf for 1½ – 2 hours. Leave in tin for 2 – 3 mins, turn out and cool on wire tray. Serve sliced and spread with butter.

Barbon W.I.

QUICK CUP LOAF

1 cup (½ pint) milk (275 ml)
1 cup mixed fruit
1 cup soft brown sugar

2 cups S.R. flour
1 teasp. mixed spice

Mix dry ingredients and add in milk. Place in a 2 lb loaf tin and bake at 350°F for 1 hour.

Preston Patrick & Preston Richard W.I.

SPICY TEA BREAD

10 oz. S.R. flour (275 g)   1 large egg – beaten
4 oz. soft brown sugar (125 g)   6 tblsp. milk
6 oz. sultanas (175 g)   1 level teasp. mixed spice
2 oz. mixed chopped peel (50 g)   ½ level teasp. each cinnamon
2 oz. margarine (50 g)   and ginger
6 oz. syrup (175 g)

Mix together all dry ingredients. Melt margarine and syrup gently and add to dry ingredients with egg and milk. Transfer to a 2 lb loaf tin and bake at 325°F for 1½ hrs approx.

Rampside W.I.

TROPICAL TEA BREAD

6 oz. dried tropical fruit and   4 oz butter or margarine (125 g)
   nut mix (175 g)   2 eggs
8 oz. S.R. flour (225 g)   3 oz soft brown sugar (75 g)
¼ teasp. salt   ¼ teasp. vanilla essence
5 tblsp. milk   2 tblsp. clear honey

Set oven at 350°F/Gas Mark 4. Grease and line 2 lb loaf tin. Sieve together flour and salt and rub in butter or margarine until like fine breadcrumbs. Mix in roughly chopped tropical mix and sugar then make a well in centre of mixture for the eggs, milk and vanilla essence. Mix to a soft dropping consistency, adding honey, and extra milk if needed. Turn into tin and smooth top. Bake for about 1 hour (until a skewer comes out clean), then turn onto a wire rack and leave to cool. Store in an airtight container, it is better if kept a few days. Will freeze.

Milnthorpe W.I.

WALNUT & ORANGE TEA BREAD

10 oz. S.R. flour (275 g)   2 teasp. finely-grated orange rind
4 oz. soft brown sugar (125 g)   1 large egg – beaten
4 oz. walnuts, chopped (125 g)   4 tblsp. milk
2 oz. margarine (50 g)   2 tblsp. orange juice
6 oz. golden syrup (175 g)

Melt margarine and syrup gently. Stir into dry ingredients with egg, milk and orange juice. Put into a 2 lb loaf tin and bake at 325°F for 1¼ hrs.

Staveley W.I.

Cakes

Alternative Fruit Cake
Banana Cake 1
Banana Cake 2
Batch Cake
Boiled Fruit Cake
Carrot & Coconut Cake
Carrot & Fruit Cake
Chocolate & Cherry Cake
Chocolate Cake
  with Cheese Frosting
Chocolate Cake with
  crushed hazelnuts
Chocolate Cake -
  Quick & Easy
Chocolate Chip Cake
Chocolate Sponge Cake
Cinnamon Streudal Cake
Coconut Cake
Coconut Fruit Cake
Coffee Cake
Coffee Fudge Cake
Devil's Food Cake
Fatless Sponge Cake
Fridge Cake
Fruit Cake – Quick & Easy

Genoa Cake
Granny's Mincemeat Cake

Grasmere Cake
Icebox Cake
Jap Special
Lemon Cake
Lemon Yogurt Cake
Macaroon Cake
Marbled Almond Cake
Marmalade Cake
Meringue Cake
Milk Fruit Cake
Mincemeat Fruit Cake 1
Mincemeat Fruit Cake 2
Murrumbidgee Cake
Newfy Nip
New Zealand Sultana Cake
Orange Drizzle Cake
Orange & Walnut Cake
Oslo Apple Cake
Pineapple Cake – Microwave
Pineapple Fruit Cake
Quick & Easy Sponge Cake
Rich Almond Cake
Sandwich Cake
Simnel Cake
Sultana, Cherry &
  Almond Cake
Tosca Cake
Wholemeal Fruit Cake

ALTERNATIVE FRUIT CAKE

8 oz. chopped, stoned prunes (225 g)
4 oz. dried apricots (125 g)   6 oz. soft dark brown sugar (175 g)
4 oz. halved glacé cherries (125 g) 6 oz. unsalted butter (175 g)
4 oz. large seedless raisins (125 g) 8 oz. mixture of chopped (225 g)
8 oz. wholemeal S. R. flour (225 g)   walnuts and hazelnuts
2 oz. brandy or rum (50 g)   3 large eggs
½ whole nutmeg   Good pinch of salt

Put all fruit in a bowl, pour brandy or rum over, stir, cover and leave overnight.

NEXT DAY

Prepare an 8/9" tin. Set oven 350°F. Place all dry ingredients in a large bowl, mix well. Cut butter into pieces and rub into flour mixture. Stir in fruit and nuts. In another bowl, whisk eggs until frothy and then stir into the mixture. Put into tin, place in centre of oven. After ½ hour, turn oven down to 300°F and bake for another 1½ to 1¾ hrs, or until cooked. If getting too brown, place a piece of greaseproof over the top.

Arnside W.I.

BANANA CAKE – 1

3 overripe bananas   1 cup of sugar
2-3 oz. margarine (50–75 g)   1½ cups S.R. flour
1 teasp. baking powder   1 egg
½ teasp. bicarb of soda   Pinch of salt

Mash bananas in large bowl. Mix sugar and bananas together with a fork. Add beaten egg. Add all dry ingredients at intervals. Gently stir in melted margarine. Place in greased 1 lb loaf tin or deep round tin. Cook on Gas Mark 5/170°C for 1 hour. Turn out and cool on wire tray, can be served buttered.

Milnthorpe W.I.

BANANA CAKE – 2

4 oz. porridge oats (125 g)   1 egg
4 oz. brown sugar (soft) (125 g)   2-3 bananas
4 oz. soft margarine (125 g)

Beat together all the ingredients, except the bananas. Spread half of the mixture into a greased 7" round tin, cover with a layer of sliced banana then finish with a layer of mixture. Bake at 180°C/350°F/ Gas Mark 4, for 45 minutes, until firm. This can also be eaten hot with cream or ice-cream.

Cliburn W.I.

BATCH CAKE

8 oz. S.R. flour (225 g)
Pinch salt (optional)
3 oz. lard or dripping (75 g)

3 oz. sugar (75 g)
4 oz. mixed fruit and peel (125 g)
milk to mix

Sieve flour and salt, rub in fat. Stir in sugar and fruit and mix to a sticky dough with milk. Spread onto a greased baking tin, round or oval 2" deep. Sprinkle with sugar, if liked. Bake in a hot oven about 20–30 mins.

Crook W.I.

BOILED FRUIT CAKE

¼ pt. milk (150 ml)
4 oz. margarine (125 g)
8 oz. brown sugar (225 g)
1 lb. mixed dried fruit (450 g)
  or fruit & nuts

12oz. S.R.flour (350 g)
2 beaten eggs
4 oz. glacé cherries (optional) (125 g)
1 teasp. mixed spice

Put the milk, margarine, sugar and dried fruit and nuts into a saucepan and bring to the boil and cool. Beat in the rest of the ingredients and place in a fairly large greased and lined cake tin approx. 7/8", bake at 250–300°F (130–150°C) for about two hours, until a skewer comes out cleanly when the cake is tested.

Grasmere W.I.

CARROT AND COCONUT CAKE

6 oz. caster sugar (175 g)
2 rounded tblsp. honey
8 oz. soft margarine (225 g)
3 large eggs
6 oz. wholemeal S.R. flour (175 g)

10 oz. grated carrot (275 g)
4 oz. dessicated coconut (125 g)
4 oz. chopped walnuts (125 g)
1 teasp. ground spice
½ teasp. salt

Put honey, margarine and sugar in a bowl. Whisk until well blended. Whisk in eggs, one at a time. Continue whisking until the mixture is light and frothy. Mix spice and flour and then add to egg mixture, a little at a time. *Stir* in grated carrot and coconut and walnuts. Pour into prepared 7"-8" tin. Bake in preheated oven 325oF for 1½ to 1¾ hours, or until cooked. If getting too brown, place a piece of greaseproof paper on top.

Arnside W.I.

CARROT AND FRUIT CAKE

4 oz. soft brown sugar (125 g) 2 teasp. baking powder
6 oz. carrot finely grated (175 g) 4 oz. butter or margarine (125 g)
2 oz. dates, chopped (50 g) 4 oz. raisins (125 g)
6 tbls. honey or syrup ¼ pt. Water (150 ml)
1 egg, beaten ¾ teasp. ground nutmeg
4 oz. wholemeal flour (125 g) 4 oz. P. flour (125 g)

Mix sugar, honey or syrup, carrot, raisins, dates, nutmeg, butter or margarine, and water together in a saucepan. Bring to boil and simmer for 5 mins. Turn into a mixing bowl and leave until cold. Stir in the egg. Mix in the flours and baking powder thoroughly. Turn the mixture into a greased roasting tin and bake for 55 to 60 mins or until firm to the touch. 180°C/350°F/Gas Mark 4.

Ravenstonedale & Newbiggin-on-Lune W.I.

CHOCOLATE AND CHERRY CAKE

6 oz. S.R. flour (175 g) 4 oz. sugar (125 g)
2 oz. ground almonds (50 g) 4 oz. margarine (125 g)
2 oz. cherries (50 g) 2 eggs, beaten with 4 tblsp. milk
4 oz. chocolate bar (125 g) and 12 drops vanilla essence

Mix flour with chopped cherries and chocolate, cut into small squares. Beat sugar and margarine to a cream, stir in beaten liquids and flour mixture (alternately, a little at a time) and mix thoroughly. Use a well-greased 6"tin (3" deep) and bake in a moderate oven (350°F to 375°F) for about 1½ hours.

Arnside W.I.

27

CHOCOLATE CAKE WITH CHEESE FROSTING

¼ lb unsalted butter (125 g)　　2 eggs, beaten
2 oz. chocolate powder (50 g)　　1 teasp. vanilla essence
1 teacupful sugar　　　　　　　8 oz. S.R. flour (225 g)
½ teacupful milk　　　　　　　1 teasp. mixed spice

Beat butter until soft. Beat in chocolate powder. Stir in sugar, milk, eggs and vanilla. Sift in flour and spices. Beat hard for several minutes. Divide equally between two greased 6" layer tins. Bake in moderately hot oven 400°F for 15–20 minutes. Cool on wire rack. Put together with chocolate filling. Cover with cheese frosting and decorate.

CHOCOLATE FILLING

¼ teacupful chocolate powder　　¼ teacupful milk
¼ teacupful caster sugar　　　　vanilla essence
½ level teasp. cornflour

Mix dry ingredients. Stir in milk. Cook until thick, stirring constantly. Leave to cool. Flavour with sufficient vanilla essence, to taste.

CHEESE FROSTING

1½ oz. soft cheese (40 g)　　　1 oz. melted chocolate (25 g)
2 tbls. milk　　　　　　　　　1 teacupful sifted icing sugar

Mash cheese and stir in milk, chocolate and sugar. Beat until smooth. Use a palette knife to ice the cake.

Kendal Strickland W.I.

CHOCOLATE CAKE WITH CRUSHED HAZELNUTS

8 oz. sugar (225 g)　　　　　　2 eggs
4 oz. P. flour (125 g)　　　　　2 oz. hazelnuts (50 g)
　preferably wholemeal　　　　　crushed with skins
½ teasp. baking powder　　　　4 oz. melted butter (125 g)
4 tbls. cocoa or margarine

Mix all dry ingredients thoroughly, add eggs, just break them into mixture; mix well, finally stir in the melted butter, pour into either an 8" square or 8" round baking tin. Bake for 30 mins, at 375°F. Cut into squares or wedges while still warm; cool on wire rack.

Killington W.I.

CHOCOLATE CAKE — QUICK & EASY

4 oz. S.R. flour (125 g)　　　　1 tbls. cocoa
1 teasp. baking powder　　　　l teasp. coffee powder
4 oz. soft margarine (125 g)　　3 tbls. warm water
4 oz. sugar (125 g)　　　　　　2 eggs

Mix all ingredients together. Put into greased sandwich cake tin. Moderate oven – 20 mins. Fill with chocolate butter cream, or thick whipped cream.

Selside W.I.

CHOCOLATE CHIP CAKE

4 oz. S.R. flour (125 g)   1 oz ground almonds (25 g)
4 oz. margarine (125 g)   2 tblsp. chocolate chips
4 oz. sugar (125 g)   2 eggs
1 oz. coconut (25 g)

Cream margarine and sugar, beat in eggs and add dry ingredients with a drop of hot water, bake 350°F for ¾ hr.

Klllington W.I.

CHOCOLATE SPONGE CAKE

3 oz. S.R. flour (sieved twice) (75 g)   3 eggs
1 oz. cocoa (25 g)   3 tblsp. cooking oil (warmed)
4 oz. granulated sugar (125 g)

Whisk eggs and sugar until thick and creamy (4-5 mins). Fold in the flour, then fold in the warm oil. Grease well (with oil), one 8" deep tin or two shallow tins. Bake at 350°F. Alternatively 4 oz. S.R. flour may be used to make a plain sponge, leaving out the cocoa.

Cliburn W.I.

CINNAMON STREUDAL CAKE

8 oz. S.R. flour (225 g)   Grated rind of ½ lemon
4 oz. butter or margarine (125 g)   1 egg
2 oz. seedless raisins (optional) (50 g)   3 oz. soft brown sugar (75 g)
1 level teasp. baking powder   ¼ pint milk (150 ml)

TOPPING
3 level tblsp. plain flour   2 oz. soft brown sugar (50 g)
1 level teasp. ground cinnamon   l oz. finely chopped walnuts (25 g)
1 oz. butter or margarine (25 g)

Sift flour and cinnamon in a bowl and add butter and sugar until crumbly. Add walnuts and set aside.

SPONGE

Sift the flour and baking powder and rub in the butter. Stir in the sugar, grated lemon rind and raisins. Lightly mix the egg and milk and add all at once to the dry ingredients. Stir with a wooden spoon until the ingredients are blended then beat until smooth. Turn into a 9" square tin and level top. Sprinkle with the topping mixture before cooking for 30 to 35 minutes at 375°F/190°C/Gas mark 5. Cool for 5 minutes before turning out.

Pooley Bridge & District W.I.

COCONUT CAKE

2 oz. coconut (50 g)(soaked in ¼ pint (150 ml) cold milk for 2 hours)
6 oz. sugar (175 g)   2 eggs
4 oz. margarine (125 g)   8 oz. S.R. flour (225 g)

Cream together margarine and sugar. Slowly add beaten eggs and fold in flour. Lastly add coconut and milk mixture. Put into a greased and lined 8" cake tin and bake for 1¼ hours at Gas Mark 2/300°F/150°C.

Barbon W.I.

COCONUT FRUIT CAKE

4 oz. soft margarine (125 g)   8 oz. S.R. flour (225 g)
4 oz. soft brown sugar (125 g)   2 small eggs (beaten)
4 oz. coconut (125 g)   8 fl. oz. milk (230 ml)
8 oz. sultanas (225 g)   vanilla essence

Put coconut and milk into a saucepan and simmer until milk is soaked up – cool. Mix margarine and sugar, add beaten eggs, coconut mixture, sultanas, flour and vanilla essence. Bake approx.1¼ hours at 325°F in a lined 8" round cake tin.

Crosthwaite & Lyth W.I.

COFFEE CAKE

6 oz. S.R. flour (175 g)   3 medium eggs
Pinch of salt   1 tblsp. coffee granules
1 teasp. baking powder   dissolved in 1 tblsp. boiling water
4 oz. butter (125 g)   1 tblsp. milk
6 oz. light brown sugar (175 g)

Cream butter and sugar, add eggs alternately with the sifted flour, salt, and baking powder. Add coffee solution and milk. Bake at 375°F.

Eden Valley W.I. Market

COFFEE FUDGE CAKE

2 oz. All Bran or Bran Buds (50 g) 2 large eggs
½ pint milk (150 ml)   4 oz. S.R. flour (125 g)
4 oz. caster sugar (125 g)   4 oz. margarine (125 g)

ICING
2 oz. margarine (50 g)   1 tblsp. water
1 tblsp. coffee essence   6 oz. icing sugar (175 g)

Soak All-Bran in milk. Beat sugar and margarine. Add eggs and flour. Mix in the All-Bran mixture. Cook on Gas Mark 4/350°F for approximately 50 mins.

For the icing melt margarine, coffee and water together. Remove from the heat and beat in icing sugar. Allow to cool, beating now and then until it thickens. (Sufficient for both top and middle).

Crook W.I.

DEVIL'S FOOD CAKE

6 oz. P. flour (175 g)   4 oz. margarine (125 g)
¼ teasp. baking powder   10 oz. caster sugar (275 g)
¼ teasp. bicarbonate of soda   2 medium eggs
2 oz. cocoa (50 g)   3½ fluid oz. water (100 ml)

Heat oven to 350°F. Well grease two 8" sandwich tins with melted fat, line bases with greased greaseproof paper. Sift flour, baking powder, bicarbonate of soda and cocoa. Cream the margarine and sugar together until light, beat in whole eggs one at a time, adding a dessert spoon of the flour mixture with each. Fold in the remainder of the flour mixture alternately with the water. When smooth, divide equally between the tins, bake in the centre of the oven 50–60 minutes, leave in tins for 5 minutes then cool on wire rack. Halve, sandwich the four layers and coat the sides with whipped double cream. Make icing with 12 oz. (350 g) icing sugar and a little warm water added by teaspoonfuls, spread over the top and leave until set.

Levens W.I.

FATLESS SPONGE CAKE

3 eggs or ½ lb in weight (225 g)   4 oz. P. flour (125 g)
4 oz. caster sugar (125 g)

Whisk eggs and sugar until thick and creamy (about 15 minutes). Sieve flour twice and fold gently into mixture. Turn into a deep 8" round cake tin which has been greased and dusted with flour. Bake in a slow oven for about 45–60 minutes or until firm.

Preston Patrick & Preston Richard W.I.

FRIDGE CAKE

8 oz. plain chocolate (225 g)   12 oz. Digestive or Nice biscuits (375 g)
8 oz. butter (225 g)   8 oz. mixed walnuts, angelica (225g)
3 oz. icing sugar (75 g)   cherries and raisins chopped
2 eggs

Oil the tin. Break chocolate and put in pan with butter until blended. Beat in icing sugar then the eggs. Crush half biscuits and stir in with nuts etc. Put a row of biscuits in base of tin, spoon some mixture on top and then layer another row of biscuits. Continue until all are used. Place in fridge.

Casterton W.I.

FRUIT CAKE – QUICK & EASY

8 oz. S.R. flour (225 g)
6 oz. soft margarine (175 g)
6 oz. soft brown sugar (175 g)
3 level tbls. marmalade

12 oz. mixed dried fruit (375 g)
3 eggs
2 oz. glacé cherries -quartered (50 g)
2 tbls, milk

Put all ingredients into a bowl and mix until well blended. Divide mixture between two 1 lb loaf tins already lined with greaseproof paper. Bake at 325°F/160°C/Gas Mark 3 for about 1¼ hours. Cool in tin for 10 minutes and then turn out. Eat one cake – freeze the other.

Appleby W.I.

GENOA CAKE

4 oz. sultanas (125 g)
4 oz. caster sugar (125)
1 oz. candied peel (25 g)
4 oz. butter or margarine (125 g)

6 oz. S.R. flour (175 g)
Grated rind and juice ½ lemon
2 eggs
½ oz. almonds for top of cake

Cream butter and sugar, add other ingredients alternately with well beaten eggs. Line and grease 7" square tin. Bake middle of oven Gas Mark 3-4 for 40–50 minutes. Do not overbake, just firm to the touch.

Allithwaite W.I.

GRANNY'S MINCEMEAT CAKE

4 oz. caster sugar (125 g)
4 oz. margarine (125 g)
1 egg
2 oz. P. flour (50 g)

3 oz. ground almonds (75 g)
4 oz. mincemeat (125 g)
Pinch of mixed spice

Blend the sugar and margarine, gradually adding the egg. Fold in the flour and ground almonds and mixed spice. Lastly fold in the mincemeat. Place in well greased and floured 1 lb loaf tin. Flatten top and sprinkle with sugar or flaked almonds. Bake for 50–60 minutes. Gas Mark 5/375°F.

Milnthorpe W.I. Market

GRASMERE CAKE

12 oz. wholemeal flour – plain (350 g)
1 teasp. mixed spice
1½ teasp. bicarbonate of soda
6 oz. soya margarine (175 g)
½ pt. milk plus 1 tblsp. (275 ml)

6 oz. currants (175 g)
3 oz. sultanas (75 g)
1 tblsp. lemon juice
6 oz. Demerara sugar (175 g)

Sift flour and spice and bicarbonate of soda. Rub in margarine and add sugar and fruit. Mix lemon juice with milk (this will sour). Add milk and lemon to flour and fruit. Stir well and leave overnight. Bake next day 1¾ to 2 hrs, 325°F. Use oblong tin approx. 9½" × 6½".

Kendal Romney W.I.

ICEBOX CAKE

8 oz. Digestive biscuits (225 g) 2 oz. chopped walnuts (50 g)
4 oz. butter or margarine (125 g) 1 large egg
5 oz. light brown sugar (150 g) Vanilla essence
A little butter icing and whole walnuts to decorate

Break the biscuits into small pieces and put in a large bowl. Melt butter in a saucepan and add the sugar and beaten egg, mixing until the sugar has dissolved. Stir well and cook until the mixture bubbles for one minute. Add the nuts and vanilla essence, pour over the biscuits. Mix well until coated. Press into a 7½" tin, leave to set in refrigerator until firm. Turn out and cover top with butter icing decorate with whole walnuts.

Ravenstonedale & Newbiggin-on-Lune W.I.

JAP SPECIAL

4 oz. ground almonds (125 g) 8 oz. caster sugar (225 g)
2 egg whites   1 Victoria sandwich
Pinch of cream of tartar   Vanilla butter icing

Whisk egg whites and cream of tartar until very stiff. Whisk in 4 oz (125 g) caster sugar. Mix together remaining 4 oz (125 g) sugar and ground almonds. Blend into meringue mixture with metal spoon. Spread or pipe two circles onto well-greased and floured tin. Bake at 350°F for about 30 minutes. Allow to cool. Make a victoria sandwich cake the same size as the two meringues. Beat butter and icing sugar to make butter icing. Cut sandwich cake in two and, beginning with the cake, put alternate layers of cake and meringue, sandwiched with butter icing. Coat sides with butter icing and roll in cake crumbs or nuts. Keep at least a week before cutting.

Pooley Bridge & District W.I.

LEMON CAKE

6 oz. butter or margarine (175 g) 2 tblsp. boiling water
6 oz. caster sugar (175 g)   2 eggs
6 oz S.R. flour (175 g)   Rind of 1 temon
TOPPING
Juice of 1 lemon   3 oz. caster sugar (75 g)

Cream butter and sugar, beat in eggs, add S.R. flour, grated rind of lemon and boiling water. Put cake in tin that has been lined slightly above the rim with greaseproof paper. Bake in moderate oven 325°F/160°C. Beat caster sugar with juice of lemon and pour over cake immediately it is taken from oven and leave in tin to cool.

Preston Patrick & Preston Richard W.I.

LEMON YOGHURT CAKE

1 pot natural yoghurt (150 g)   1 large lemon
1 pot corn oil   3 large eggs
3 pots caster sugar   Icing sugar
4 pots S.R.flour

Into a bowl put the yoghurt and grated rind and juice of the lemon. Using the carton as a measure add the oil and sugar then add the lightly beaten eggs. Bind together and add sifted flour and beat again. Put into two base-lined sandwich tins and bake in centre of oven at 160°C until firm (about 45 minutes). When cold ice with lemon icing. Orange may be used instead of lemon.

Urswick W.I.

MACAROON CAKE

3 oz butter (75 g)   2 egg yolks
3 oz. sugar (75 g)   milk to mix
4 oz. S.R. flour (125 g)

TOPPING
2 egg whites   3 oz. caster sugar (75 g)
3 oz desiccated coconut (75 g)

Preheat oven to 350°F. Cream butter and sugar, mix in egg yolks. Add flour and milk to soft consistency. Put in to 7" greased and lined deep cake tin. Whip egg whites until stiff, add sugar and coconut and spread on top of cake. Bake for 50 minutes.

Kendal W.I. Market

MARBLED ALMOND CAKE

3 oz. ground almonds (75 g)   8 oz. cherries, halved (225 g)
7½ oz. caster sugar (210 g)   1 oz. desiccated coconut (25 g)
5 oz. butter or margarine (150 g) 3 eggs, beaten
5 oz. P. flour (150 g)

Mix the ground almonds and 3 oz. (75 g) of the sugar with 2 tblsp. of egg to a paste – set aside. Beat butter and remaining sugar until light and creamy. Then beat in eggs altogether with half the flour. Fold in rest of flour before cherries and coconut. Turn half the mixture into a 7" tin then roll the almond paste to fit the tin and place on top pressing down gently. Cover with remainder of cake mixture. Bake at 325°F for 1½ hours.
Leave in tin for 5 minutes before turning out.

Underbarrow W.I.

MARMALADE CAKE

6 oz. flour (175 g)	1 egg
3 oz. sugar (75 g)	2 tblsp. milk
2 oz. butter (50 g)	1 good tblsp. marmalade
½ teasp. baking powder	

In mixer, mix dry ingredients then add liquid and lastly marmalade. In processor, process all ingredients together. Bake in fairly hot oven for about 1 hour.

Underbarrow W.I.

MERINGUE CAKE (for a special occasion)

6 egg whites	¼ teasp. ground cinnamon
8 oz. caster sugar (225 g)	Pinch allspice
5 tblsp. cocoa	Pinch powdered cloves
Vanilla essence	Pinch cream of tartar
3 oz. flour (75 g)	

FILLING
3 tblsp. sour cream	Vanilla essence
3 tblsp. brown sugar	1 oz. chopped nuts (25 g)
1 tblsp. butter	2 oz. shredded coconut (50 g)

Whisk egg whites and then beat in cocoa, sugar, spices and vanilla. Mix in flour, stirring as little as possible. Pour mixture in a pair of greased loaf tins and bake in a moderate oven for 30 minutes or until the edges come away from the tins. Cool.

TO COOK FILLING
Mix sugar and cream in a saucepan and boil slowly for 15 minutes. Add vanilla and butter and cook until it thickens. Cool, add nuts and sandwich between the 2 cakes. The cake should be served cut into slices 2" thick, it will cut more easily when it is cool.

Ulpha & Seathwaite W.I.

MILK FRUIT CAKE

½ lb margarine (225 g)	½ lb S.R. flour (225 g)
½ lb soft dark brown sugar (225 g)	1 lb mixed fruit (450 g)
2 eggs	1 small tin Carnation Milk

Cream margarine and sugar, add eggs, then flour and fruit. Last of all add Carnation Milk. Bake Gas Mark 2/150°C/300°F for 1 hour or longer until firm. Keeps well.

Urswick W.I.

MINCEMEAT FRUIT CAKE

8 oz. S.R. flour 225 g)   Jar mincemeat
5 oz. soft brown sugar (150 g)   3 oz. mixed dried fruit (75 g)
5 oz. margarine (150 g)   3 eggs

Cream margarine and sugar. Add beaten eggs and flour alternately. Finally beat in dried fruit and mincemeat. Grease and line an 8" square cake tin. Bake in a moderate oven (350°F/180°C) for 1½ hours.

Soulby W.I.

MINCEMEAT FRUIT CAKE – 2

10 oz. S.R. flour (275 g)   2 oz. chopped cherries (50 g)
8 oz. soft margarine (225 g)   4 eggs
7 oz. soft brown sugar (200 g)   Jar mincemeat
2 oz. chopped peanuts (50 g)

Beat all ingredients together. Put in a greased and lined 9" cake tin and sprinkle with 1 tablespoon Demerara sugar. Bake at 350°F for 45 minutes.

Silverdale W.I.

MURRUMBIDGEE CAKE

7 oz. whole brazil nuts (200 g)   ½ level teasp. baking powder
5 oz. walnut halves (150 g)   ½ level teasp. salt
8 oz. stoned dates (225 g)   5 oz. caster sugar (150 g)
3 oz. chopped peel (candied) (75 g) 3 large eggs
6 oz. glacé cherries (175 g)   1 teasp. vanilla essence
3 oz. seedless raisins (75 g)   plus Brandy, Rum or other
Grated rind of 1 lemon   liqueur or other spirit
3 oz. P. flour (75 g)

Line 8" round or square tin with Bakewell or buttered greaseproof paper. Heat oven to 300°F/150°C. Sift dry ingredients together and make into batter with the beaten eggs and vanilla. Add mixed nuts and fruit. Put into tin and smooth down the top. Bake 1½ to 2 hours protecting with greaseproof paper if browning too fast. Test with skewer, when cooked, cool for 10 minutes, then turn out and leave until cold. Pierce base of cake with thin knitting needle and pour 2 tablespoons of chosen spirits over the base. Wrap cake in greaseproof paper and then in foil or cling film. Add spirits every week for 4 weeks. Store for 1 to 2 months before eating.

Appleby W.I.

NEWFY NIP

Beat 2 eggs.
Add cup of sugar (pref. brown).
Beat again.
Add 1 cup chopped walnuts.
Add 1 cup of chopped dates (or more).
5 level tblsp. of sifted flour (½ teasp. baking powder if not S.R.).
Good pinch salt (cinnamon too if liked).
Cook in moderate oven.
Cut when cool and sprinkle with icing sugar.

This quantity fills two sandwich tins.

Underbarrow W.I.

NEW ZEALAND SULTANA CAKE

8 oz butter (225 g)	2 lb sultanas (900 g)
8 oz. caster sugar (225 g)	4 large eggs
12 oz. plain flour (350 g)	

Cream butter and sugar. Beat in eggs one at a time, do not add extra liquid (e.g. milk). Fold in pre-cleaned sultanas. Sieve flour and fold in to creamed mixture (do *not* add salt) – a fairly stiff mixture. Bake in greased and lined tin (7" sq. or 8" diameter) 350°F for 30 mins and at 300°F for 2 hrs (Gas Mark 4 for 30 mins Gas Mark 3 for 2hrs).

Dentdale W.I.

ORANGE DRIZZLE CAKE

6 oz. S.R. flour(175 g)	2 eggs
6 oz. caster sugar (175 g)	½ cup of milk
4 oz. margarine (125 g)	Rind of 1 orange

Cream sugar and margarine, beat in eggs, add flour, milk and rind. 350°F for 1 hour.

TOPPING
Juice of orange and 2 oz. (50 g) of sugar mixed together. When cake is cooked, remove from oven and pour mixture over top. A lemon may be substituted for the orange.

Arnside W.I.

ORANGE AND WALNUT CAKE

8 oz. S.R. flour (225 g)	3 large eggs
6 oz. butter (175 g)	1 tblsp. concentrated orange juice
1 oz. mixed peel (25 g)	1 teasp. salt
6 oz. caster sugar (175 g)	2 oz. walnuts – chopped (50 g)
Rind of 1 orange	

Cream butter and sugar, add eggs alternately with the sifted flour and salt. Blend in the rest of the ingredients. Put mixture into a greased 7" cake tin and bake for 1½ hours at 150°C. May be iced using 8 oz. (225g) icing sugar and 2-3 tblsp. concentrated orange juice, and decorated with walnuts.

Eden Valley W.I. Market

OSLO APPLE CAKE

FOR APPLE LAYER

3 large cooking apples	1 teasp. grated lemon rind
2 oz. sugar (50 g)	1 tblsp. lemon juice

Peel, core and slice apples, cook with the sugar, rind and juice. Add a little water if necessary but keep a firm, almost dry mixture. Strain when soft to remove surplus moisture and cool thoroughly.

FOR CAKE LAYER

8 oz. S.R. flour (225 g)	4 oz. caster sugar (125 g)
4 oz. margarine (125 g)	1 small egg

Sieve the flour, rub in the margarine and add half the sugar with the egg. Knead together then add rest of the sugar. Roll or press out two-thirds of the dough to an 8" round. Place in a well-greased loose-based deep sandwich tin. Top with the apple mixture. Roll out the rest of the dough, cut into strips and make a lattice design on top of the apples. Bake in the centre of the oven at 350–375°F for 40 minutes. Eat hot or cold but serve fresh. This is delicious with fresh cream.

Levens W.I.

PINEAPPLE CAKE – MICROWAVE

½ oz. unsalted butter (10 g)   4 oz. unsalted butter (125 g)
1 tblsp soft brown sugar   4 oz. S.R. flour (125 g)
1 small tin pineapple chunks   2 beaten eggs
Few glacé cherries and/   2 tblsp. water
   or angelica

Lightly grease 7" soufflé dish. Sprinkle bottom and sides with brown sugar. Drain the pineapple chunks and layer the dish with them in an agreeable pattern, together with glacé cherries and/or angelica. Mix remaining ingredients. Beat well. Pour over pineapple. Cook on HIGH for 6 minutes. Stand for 5 minutes before turning out.

FILLING
½ pint of milk (275 ml)   1 beaten egg
1 oz. cornflour (25 g)   ½ teasp. vanilla essence
1 oz. sugar (25 g)

Mix cornflour, egg and vanilla to a smooth paste. Boil sugar and milk and pour over paste; cook on medium heat, stirring all the time until thick. Allow to cool but not set. When cake is absolutely cold, split into three and spread the filling between each piece.
NOTE: For better colour of cake, substitute one rounded teasp. of custard powder for one rounded teaspoon of flour.

Kendal Strickland W.I.

PINEAPPLE FRUIT CAKE

6 oz. soft brown sugar (175 g)   4 oz. glace cherries (125 g)
1 tin crushed pineapple (376 g size)
12 oz. mixed dried fruit (350 g)   4 oz. butter (125 g)

Put all ingredients in pan and bring to the boil. When cool add 2 eggs and 8 oz. S.R. flour (225 g). If desired, add a little rum, spice and cinnamon.
Mix together and bake for 1 hour 40 minutes at 300°F/150°C in an 8" greased and lined tin. (Best if kept for 1 week before eating).

Grasmere W.I.

QUICK & EASY SPONGE CAKE

2 eggs (large)   ½ teacup *boiling* milk
1 teacup caster sugar   walnut-sized piece of butter
1 teacup S.R. flour

Beat eggs and sugar together until fairly thick but do not over-beat, fold in flour. Melt butter in hot milk and bring to the boil and fold into the mixture carefully but thoroughly. Pour into 2 greased and floured tins. Bake at 375°F.

Arnside W.I.

RICH ALMOND CAKE

4 oz. butter (125 g)
3 oz. ground almonds (75 g)
1½ oz. S.R. flour (40 g)

5 oz. caster sugar (150 g)
3 eggs
Almond essence

Grease and flour 7" cake tin. Set oven 350°F/180°C/Gas Mark 4. Soften butter, add sugar, beat well until soft and light. Add eggs, one at a time with tablespoon of flour and ground almonds. Beat well. Fold in the rest of the mixture and add the essence. Bake for 40–45 minutes. Dust with caster sugar to serve.

Stainmore W.I.

SANDWICH CAKE

10 oz. S.R. flour (275 g)
8 oz. soft margarine (225 g)

8 oz. caster sugar (225 g)
4 eggs, beaten

Mix altogether by hand for 1 minute or 30 to 40 seconds by machine. Alternatives: Juice and grated rind of 1 lemon. Juice and grated rind of 1 orange.
2 oz. (50 g) cocoa powder instead of 2 oz. (50 g) of flour.

Tebay W.I.

SIMNEL CAKE

6 oz. margarine (175 g)
6 oz. caster sugar (175 g)
3 eggs
1 tblsp. milk
2 oz. glacé cherries (50 g)
1 oz. marmalade (25 g)

1 oz. chopped almonds (25 g)
8 oz. P. flour (225 g)
3 rounded teasp. mixed spice
6 oz. currants (175 g)
4 oz. sultanas (125 g)
Marzipan

Cream margarine and sugar. Beat in eggs one at a time. Sieve flour and spice, fold in. Add milk, almonds, sultanas, cherries and marmalade. Mix well together. Put half the mixture into a 7" tin, put a round of marzipan on top and cover with the rest of the cake mixture. Bake in a slow oven for 2-2½ hrs (300°F/150°C/Gas Mark 2), cover with marzipan when cold.

Arnside W.I.

SULTANA, CHERRY AND ALMOND CAKE

10 oz. S.R. flour (275 g)
8 oz. butter or margarine (225 g)
8 oz. sugar (225 g)
12 oz. sultanas (350 g)

2 oz. cherries (50 g)
2 oz. ground almonds (50 g)
4 eggs
½ teasp. baking powder

Cream butter and sugar, add eggs and flour alternately (beating well) lastly ground almonds, fruit and baking powder. Bake in moderate oven – 325°F/160°C.

Preston Patrick & Preston Richard W.I.

TOSCA CAKE

5 oz. caster sugar (150 g)
4 oz. margarine (125 g)
5 oz. flour (150 g)

1½ teasp. baking powder
2 tblsp. milk
2 eggs

TOPPING
2 oz. butter (50 g)
2 oz. caster sugar (50 g)
2 oz. nuts, chopped (50 g)

1 dessp. flour
1 dessp. milk

Beat eggs and sugar, add melted margarine and stir. Fold in the sieved flour and baking powder and lastly the milk. Put into greased and floured 8" round tin, bake for 25–30 minutes at 370°F. Just before the cake finishes baking make the topping. Add all ingredients to a saucepan and bring to the boil stirring continuously. Remove the cake from the oven and spread the topping mixture over the top. Replace to oven for a further 10–15 minutes when the topping should be a nice caramel colour. Cool for 10 minutes before releasing from tin.

Garth Row & Skelmergh W.I.

WHOLEMEAL FRUIT CAKE

1 lb wholemeal S.R. flour (450 g)
1 teasp. mixed spice
6 oz. butter (rub in) (175 g)
8 oz. brown sugar (225 g)
  or black molasses

12 oz. (350 g) mixed dried fruit e.g. apricots (cut into small pieces), currants, sultanas, raisins) etc.

Soak fruit in ½ pint (275 ml) milk and 1 egg for about an hour. Mix all ingredients. Line a 12" × 8" roasting tin, place in mixture and cook for 1½ to 2 hours at 250°F or ½-1 Gas Mark.

Windermere W.I.

Tray Bakes

Almond Fingers
Almond Slices – 1
Almond Slices – 2
Almond Meringue Cake
Apple Sponge Slice
Apricot Coconut Cake
Brides Fingers
Cherry & Walnut Meringue Slices
Chinese Chews
Chocolate Biscuit Cake
Chocolate Chip Squares
Chocky Chunks
Chocolate Coconut Slice
Chocolate Cracknel
Chocolate & Date Crisp
Chocolate Fingers
Chocolate Muesli Bars
Chocolate Peppermint Squares
Chocolate Shortbread
Cinnamon & Apple Slice
Coconut & Almond Slice
Coconut Crunch
Coconut Ice Cake
Coconut Meringue Slice
Crunchy Bake
Cumberland Currant Pastry
Date Crunchies
Date Fingers
Date Flapjack

Fruit Fingers
Fruit Flapjack
Fruit & Nut Bars
Fruit & Nut Squares
Grannie's Crunch
Holly Bars
Jam Cake
Jericho Cake
Lemon Meringue Bars
Lemon Shortcake
Liesl's Whacky Cake
Mallow Delights
Margaret's Mars Bars
Marshmallow Crispies
Matilda Cake
Mincemeat Fingers
Mocha Squares
Moist Chocolate & Orange
  Squares
Non-cooking Treat
Nut & Fruit Shortbread
Oaty Currant Triangles
Paradise Cake
Rich Fruit Slices
Strabane Fingers
Sydney's Special
Tea-Time Fingers
Westmorland Currant Pasty
Westmorland Dream Cake

ALMOND FINGERS

6 oz. semolina (175 g)   Pinch salt
6 oz. S.R. flour (175 g)   ½ teaspoon almond essence
6 oz. butter or margarine (175 g)   Apricot jam
6 oz. caster sugar (175 g)   1 oz. blanched almonds (25 g)
1 egg

Rub fat into dry ingredients, add egg, divide mixture into two portions, press one half into Swiss roll tin spread with jam, put remaining paste on top of jam, decorate with almonds. Bake for approx 20mins until golden brown. Cook at 350°F/180°C/Gas Mark 4. Cool and cut into fingers.

Windermere W.I.

ALMOND SLICES – 1

2 oz. margarine (50 g)   2 oz. ground rice (50 g)
2 oz. sugar (50 g)   1 egg
2 oz. ground almonds (50 g)   1½ oz. flaked almonds (40 g)

Line a Swiss roll tin with shortcrust pastry and spread with red jam. Cream together margarine and sugar. Add ground almonds, ground rice and egg. Spread over jam. Sprinkle with 1½ oz. (40 g) flaked almonds. Bake on Gas Mark 5 for 20–25 minutes. Cut when cold.

Underbarrow W.I.

ALMOND SLICES – 2

3 oz. butter (75 g)   6 oz. S.R. flour (175 g)
Yolk of 2 eggs   Pinch salt
3 oz. caster sugar (75 g)

Cream butter and sugar. Add the yolks of 2 eggs then add the flour and salt. Spread on a flat tin and cover with raspberry jam.

FILLING
4 oz. ground almonds (125 g)   Whites of 2 eggs
6 oz. icing sugar (175 g)   Few drops of almond essence

Do not beat the egg whites but add all the ingredients to them. Spread on top of the jam. Bake in moderate oven for 25 minutes. Start at 325°F then turn down to 320°F later. Use top or middle shelf.

Urswick W.I.

ALMOND MERINGUE CAKE

3 oz. margarine (75 g)
4 oz. caster sugar (125 g)
2 egg yolks
2 tblsp. milk

Few drops almond essence
6 oz. S.R. flour (175 g)
½ teasp. salt

TOPPING
2 egg white
2 oz. coconut (50 g)
4 oz.sugar (125 g)

Few drops of almond essence
Flaked almonds

Cream sugar and margarine, beat in yolks, milk and essence. Fold in flour and salt. Grease and line Swiss roll tin. Spread mixture in tin. Beat egg whites and use sugar to make meringue mixture. Fold in coconut and essence. Spread on top of base mixture and sprinkle with flaked almonds. Bake in moderate oven (Gas Mark 3/325°F/160°C) for about 30 minutes. Leave to cool in tin. When cold, cut into slices/squares.

Kirkby Lonsdale W.I. Market

APPLE SPONGE SLICE

4 oz. S.R. flour (sieved) (125 g)
4 oz. margarine (125 g)
4 oz. caster sugar (125 g)
2 large eggs (beaten)

a few drops almond essence
2 eating apples (pineapples can
  be used)
1 oz Demerara sugar (25 g)

Lightly grease and line Swiss roll tin, grease paper also. Cream margarine and sugar, gradually add beaten eggs stirring well, add almond essence, fold in flour. Spread evenly in tin, peel and core apples, cut into 36 slices, arrange on top of mixture, sprinkle with Demerara sugar. Bake at 350°F/180°C for 40 minutes. Pineapple rings can be cut into quarters and cooked as apple.

Cliburn W.I.

APRICOT COCUNUT CAKE

1½ cups P. flour
Pinch of salt
1 cup sugar
4 oz soft margarine (125 g)

2 eggs
1 cup dessicated coconut
Few drops almond essence
Apricot jam

Cream margarine, ½ cup sugar and essence. Add 1 beaten egg. Mix well and add sifted flour and salt. Spread over a greased Swiss roll tin. Cover with jam. Beat remaining egg, add balance of sugar and coconut. Mix well and spread over mixture in tin. Bake in moderate oven 25 to 30 minutes 350°F/180°C/Gas Mark 4. When cool, cut into slices.

Crook W.I.

BRIDES FINGERS

8 oz. shortcrust pastry (225 g)   2 oz. butter (50 g)
2 oz.sugar (50 g)   4 oz. cherries (125 g)
8 digestive biscuits (crushed)   2 eggs
1 lb currants (450 g)   Glacé icing

Line a Swiss roll tin with the pastry. Cream the butter and sugar, then beat in the eggs. Add the crushed biscuits and fruit. Bake at 350°F/180°C/Gas Mark 4 for 30–45 mins. When cold decorate with glacé icing, when set cut into fingers.

Kirkby Thore W.I.

CHERRY & WALNUT MERINGUE SLICES

2 oz. brown sugar (50 g)   6 oz. S.R. flour (175 g)
3 oz. margarine (75 g)   1 teasp. vanilla essence
2 egg yolks

Cream sugar and margarine, add beaten egg yolks, flour and lastly vanilla essence. Mix together to a stiff paste. Spread evenly in a greased Swiss roll tin and flatten.

TOPPING
2 egg whites   1 cup each of glacé cherries and
4 oz. caster sugar (125 g)   walnuts (chopped)

Beat egg whites until stiff, gradually fold in sugar followed by nuts and cherries and spread evenly over base mixture. Bake in a moderate oven 350°F/180°C/Gas Mark 4 for 20–30 minutes until lightly browned and crisp.

Grasmere W.I.

CHINESE CHEWS

3 oz. margarine (75 g)   3 oz. plain flour (75 g)
5 oz. caster sugar (150 g)   10 oz. chopped dates (275 g)
2 eggs   4 oz. chopped walnuts (125 g)

Cream the margarine and sugar, and add eggs, then add the rest of the ingredients. Spread into a greased Swiss roll tin. Medium oven for about ½ hour. Remove from oven and sprinkle with extra sugar. Cut into fingers when cooled.

Underbarrow W.I.

CHOCOLATE BISCUIT CAKE

6 oz. margarine (175 g)	4 oz. raisins
1 ½ oz. cocoa or (40 g)	12 oz. cheap biscuits (350 g)
drinking chocolate	(Morning Coffee, Rich Tea)
4½ oz. syrup (125 g)	

Melt margarine, cocoa, syrup and raisins together in a pan over a low heat. Add biscuits, crushed (not too fine). Prepare a Swiss roll tin, well greased. Press the mixture into tin, when set, cover with 4 to 6 oz. (125–175 g) melted cooking chocolate. When set, cut into fingers or squares – not too big, as this is quite rich.

Preston Patrick & Preston Richard W.I.

CHOCOLATE CHIP SQUARES

4 oz. soft margarine (125 g)	1 teasp. vanilla essence
6 oz. Demerara sugar (175 g)	8 oz. S.R. flour (225 g)
1 egg	4 oz. chocolate chips (125 g)

Prepare moderate oven 350°F/180°C/Gas Mark 4. Grease a tin 11" × 7"× 1" inch deep. Place all the ingredients in a bowl and mix thoroughly. Spread the mixture in the tin and bake for 35–40 minutes until it is golden brown and has shrunk slightly from sides of tin. Leave to cool, then cut into 16 pieces. Lift out and cool on a wire rack.

Kendal Parr W.I.

CHOCKY CHUNKS

8 oz. margarine (225 g)	3 oz. coconut (75 g)
4 oz. sugar (125 g)	7 oz. P. flour (200 g)
2 teasp. cocoa	

Cream margarine and sugar. Add other ingredients, press into shallow tin. Bake for 30 minutes at 360°F.

ICING

6 oz. icing sugar (175 g)	Nut of margarine
2 teasp. cocoa tblsp.	boiling water

Mix all together and spread on cake while hot. Cool and cut.

Urswick W.I.

CHOCOLATE COCONUT SLICE

8 oz. block milk chocolate (225 g) 4 oz. dessicated coconut (125 g)
2 oz. butter or margarine (50 g)   2 oz. sultanas (50 g)
4 oz. caster sugar (125 g)   2 oz glacé cherries (50 g)
1 beaten egg

Break chocolate into pieces and melt in a basin over water. Pour into greased shallow tin 11" × 7" and allow to set. Cream fat and sugar until light and fluffy. Add beaten egg and all other ingredients. Mix well and spread out evenly over the set chocolate. Bake in a slow oven (310°F/Gas Mark 2) for approximately 45 minutes until golden brown. Take out of oven and after 5 minutes mark into pieces then leave until cold before taking out of tin.

Kendal Castle W.I.

CHOCOLATE CRACKNEL

MELT
3½ oz. margarine (75 g)   7 oz. golden syrup (200 g)

MIX
½ lb cornflakes (225 g)   5½ oz. dried milk powder (150 g)
½ oz.cocoa (10 g)

Then add melted mixture. Press quickly into greased tins and leave to set. No cooking required.

Underbarrow W.I.

CHOCOLATE AND DATE CRISP

4 oz. margarine (125 g)   1 packet dates
2 oz. sugar (50 g)   ½ lb cooking chocolate (225 g)
4 oz. Rice Krispies (125 g)

Melt margarine and cut up the dates. Mix well. Add sugar and Rice Krispies. Press into Swiss roll tin and cover with melted chocolate. Cut when cold.

Broughton Mills & Woodland W.I.

CHOCOLATE FINGERS

BISCUIT BASE

4 oz. P. flour (125 g)   2½ oz. caster sugar (60 g)
½ oz. cocoa (10 g)   beaten egg to mix (½-1 whole egg)
2½ oz. butter (60 g)

Rub butter into flour and cocoa with pinch of salt. Add sugar and enough egg to make a stiff dough. Roll out to fit an 8" × 10" baking tray and prick base. Bake for 15–20 minutes, Gas mark 4/350°F/180°C. Leave to cool.

FILLING

Small tin condensed milk   ½ lb desiccated coconut (225 g)
2 oz. margarine (50 g)   2 oz. chopped glacé cherries (50 g)
3 tbls. icing sugar

Melt condensed milk and margarine in a pan. Remove from heat and stir in icing sugar, coconut and cherries. Mix well and spread over base. Cool.

TOPPING

8 oz. cake chocolate (225 g)

Melt cake chocolate and spread over filling. Allow to cool and then cut into fingers.

Barbon W.I.

CHOCOLATE MUESLI BARS

2 oz. (50 g) butter   10 oz. (275 g) muesli
2 rounded tblsp. Set honey   8 oz. (225 g) chocolate bar

Melt the butter and honey together in a fairly large saucepan, stir in muesli, spoon into an 8" × 10" (20 × 25 cm) tin or round cake tin, lined and greased. Press down with a spoon. Place in centre of oven and bake for 20 minutes at 180°C/350°F/Gas Mark 4. Melt chocolate in pan over a very low heat, and spread over the muesli base, leave to cool then mark into bars. When quite cold, separate bars and store in an airtight container. Makes ten bars.

Lowther W.I.

CHOCOLATE PEPPERMINT SQUARES

3 oz. soft brown sugar (75 g)   2 teasp. Cocoa
6 oz. margarine (175 g)   Pinch of salt
6 oz. S.R. flour (175 g)

Cream together sugar and margarine. Stir in flour, cocoa and salt. Put mixture on a 7" × 11" baking tray and bake for 20 minutes at Gas Mark 4/350°F/180°C. Leave to cool.

TOPPING
8 oz. icing sugar (225 g)   ½ teasp. green colouring
½ teasp. peppermint essence   A little water

Mix together. Spread over base and leave to set. Melt 8 oz. (225 g) cake chocolate and pour over. Leave to set and cut into squares.

Barbon W.I.

CHOCOLATE SHORTBREAD

11 oz. P. flour (300 g)   1 oz. cocoa (25 g)
1 heaped teasp. baking powder   1 egg
½ lb sugar (225 g)   Pinch of salt
½ lb margarine (225 g)   Few drops vanilla essence

Rub fat into flour. Add everything else and mix well. Press into Swiss roll tin with wet hands. Sprinkle with extra sugar. Bake at Gas Mark 4 for 20 minutes. Cut into fingers whilst warm.

Underbarrow W.I.

CINNAMON AND APPLE SLICE 1921

4 oz. margarine (125 g)   2 eggs
4 oz. caster sugar (125 g)   2 lb sliced cooking apples (900 g)
6 oz S.R. flour (175 g)   1 teasp. ground cinnamon

Grease a 13" × 9" tin. Cream margarine and sugar. Add eggs and beat well, add sifted flour. Spread in tin and cover with rows of sliced apple, sprinkle cinnamon on top. Bake at 190°C/375°F/Gas Mark 4, for 30 minutes. Sprinkle with sugar before cake cools. This is good as a pudding also, served with custard.

Kirkby Lonsdale W.I. Market

COCONUT AND ALMOND SLICE

3 oz. P. flour (75 g)   Milk (optional)
1 oz margarine (25 g)   4 oz.-5 oz. coconut (125–150 g)
2 oz. sugar (50 g)   2 oz. flaked almonds (50 g)
1 egg (separated)   1 oz.-2 oz. apricot jam (25–50 g)

BASE

Rub fat in flour until breadcrumb-like.
Mix 1 oz. (25 g) sugar into above.
Gather together with beaten egg yolk. (If not enough to make stiff dough add a drop or two of milk).
Spread mixture onto small greased Swiss roll tin.
Flatten to edges with knuckles (as kneading).
Spread jam thinly over pastry base.

TOPPING

Beat egg white until stiff.
Add 1 oz. (25 g) sugar and whisk again.
Gently stir in coconut and 1 oz. (25 g) almond flakes.
Spread evenly over base.
Cover with remainder of flaked almonds.
Place in oven for approx. 20 mins. until golden brown, 180°C/Gas Mark 4.
Cut up into slices and allow to cool.

Milnthorpe W.I.

COCONUT CRUNCH

2 cups S.R. flour   1 cup sugar
2 cups coconut   ½ lb melted margarine (225 g)
2 cups cornflakes

Mix together or press into 12" × 8" Swiss roll tin. Bake Gas Mark 3/160°C/325°F until golden brown, may be iced or covered with chocolate. Cut into squares. Store in airtight tin.

Urswick W.I.

COCONUT ICE CAKE

4 oz. plain chocolate (125 g)   4 oz. coconut (125 g)
2 oz. margarine (50 g)   4 oz. caster sugar (125 g)
2 oz. chopped cherries (50 g)   1 egg

Line 7½" square tin. Break chocolate into a bowl over hot water. Pour into tin to set. Melt margarine and stir in coconut, sugar and cherries. Add egg and mix well. Spread over chocolate and bake Gas Mark 4/190°F/375°F for 20–25 minutes and then leave in tray overnight. Next day peel off greaseproof and cut into pieces.

Heversham W.I.

COCONUT MERINGUE SLICE

BASE

3 oz. margarine (75 g)   Few drops of vanilla essence
3 oz. caster sugar (75 g)   6 oz. S.R. flour (175 g)
2 egg yolks   ½ teasp. salt
2 tblsp. Milk

Cream margarine and sugar, beat in egg yolks, milk and essence. Fold in flour and salt. Line and grease a Swiss roll tin. Press mixture into tin.

TOPPING

2 egg whites   chopped cherries
2 oz. coconut (50 g)   chopped nuts
4 oz. caster sugar (125 g)

Beat egg whites until stiff, add coconut and sugar. Spread mixture over base and sprinkle with cherries and nuts. Bake in moderate oven 325°F about 30 minutes. When cool cut into slices and remove from tin.

Preston Patrick & Preston Richard W.I.

CRUNCHY BAKE

3 oz. Demerara sugar (75 g)   2 oz. porridge oats (50 g)
6oz. margarine (175 g)   1 oz. chopped walnuts (25 g)
1 oz. S.R. flour (25 g)   or mixed nuts
3 tbls. golden syrup   1 oz. coconut (25 g)
4 oz. crushed cornflakes (125 g)

Melt margarine, syrup and sugar in pan. Add to dry ingredients. Put into greased Swiss roll tin. Cook in moderate oven for 15–20 minutes. Cut whilst warm. Bake at 350°F/180°C/Gas Mark 4.

Selside W.I.

CUMBERLAND CURRANT PASTRY

8 oz. pastry (225 g)   1 oz. margarine (25 g)
6 oz. currants (175 g)   1 oz. ground almonds (25 g)
2 oz. mixed peel (50 g)   ½ teasp. mixed spice
4 oz. golden syrup (125 g)   2 teasp. lemon juice

Warm margarine and syrup together; stir in all the other filling ingredients. When cool, spread between two layers of pastry and cook in a hot oven.

Tebay W.I.

DATE CRUNCHIES

1 tblsp. syrup	6 oz. butter or margarine (175 g)
1 tblsp. lemon juice	8 oz. Block of dates (225 g)
4 tblsp. water	6 oz. caster sugar (175 g)
¼ level teasp. mixed spice	6 oz. semolina (175 g)
6 oz S.R. flour (175 g)	

Lightly grease 7" × 11" Swiss roll tin. Chop dates, put in saucepan with syrup, lemon juice, water and mixed spice. Cover pan and simmer for 3 minutes. Remove and beat to a spreadable consistency then leave to one side. In another pan heat margarine and when melted remove from heat and stir in the flour, sugar and semolina. Place half this mixture in tin and press into an even layer. Cover this with the date mixture and crumble the rest of the mixture over the top and press down lightly. Bake for 30 minutes, Gas Mark 3/350°F to a rich golden brown. Leave in tin for 10 minutes before cutting into squares.

Milnthorpe W.I. Market

DATE FINGERS

8 oz. chopped dates (225 g)	1 tblsp. melted margarine or butter
2 oz. chopped walnuts (50 g)	1 tblsp. hot water
3 oz. S.R. flour (75 g)	1 egg (beaten)
2 oz. sugar (50 g)	

Mix all ingredients together. Spread over well-greased flat baking tin and bake for about 25 minutes (Gas Mark 3/350°F/180°C). When cool, cut into fingers.

Burton W.I.

DATE FLAPJACK

1 lb oats (450 g)	8 heaped teasp. sugar
8 oz. hard margarine (225 g)	2 tblsp. syrup
8 oz. chopped dates (225 g)	

Melt margarine and syrup in a big saucepan. Remove from heat and mix in the rest of the ingredients. Press into a well greased Swiss roll tin. Bake for ½ hour in a moderate oven. Cut whilst warm. 350°F/180°C Gas Mark 4.

Underbarrow W.I.

FRUIT FINGERS

3 oz. butter or margarine (75 g)	4 oz. P. flour (125 g)
5 oz. sugar (150 g)	12 oz. mixed fruit (350 g)
2 eggs	

Cream butter and sugar and add eggs, beat well. Fold in flour and fruit. Spread into an 11" × 7" Swiss roll tin. Bake for about ½ hour at 350°F/180°C/ Gas Mark 4 until nicely brown and firm on top. When cold, cut into fingers.

Levens W.I.

FRUIT FLAPJACK

2 oz. glacé cherries chopped (50 g)   3 oz. soft brown sugar (75 g)
2 oz. chopped walnuts (50 g)   3 oz. golden syrup (75 g)
4 oz. margarine (125 g)   6 oz. rolled oats (175 g)

Grease a shallow 7 ½" square tin. Melt sugar, syrup and margarine in a saucepan over low heat. Stir in oats, cherries and walnuts and mix well. Bake in centre of oven for 30 minutes. Cut into squares whilst hot. Leave to cool in tin. 350°F/180°C/Gas Mark 4.

Windermere W.I.

FRUIT & NUT BARS

4 oz. dates (125 g)   2 oz. glace cherries (quartered) (50 g)
4 oz. raisins (125 g)   1 oz. chocolate powder (25 g)
2 oz. candied peel (50 g)   1 teasp. finely grated lemon peel
4 oz. hazelnuts (125 g)   1 tblsp. Masala or sweet sherry

Put first four ingredients in blender until well minced. Turn out into a mixing bowl and add remainder of ingredients. Mix. Line an 8" × 8" shallow baking tin with a sheet of rice paper. On this spread the mixture and press down making a sandwich with another sheet of rice paper. Cut into fingers.

Bowness W.I

FRUIT & NUT SQUARES

6 oz S.R. flour (175 g)   6 oz. wheatmeal flour (175 g)
¼ teasp. salt   2 oz sultanas (50 g)
8 oz. soft margarine (225 g) 2 oz. chopped walnuts (50 g)
4 oz. Demerara sugar (125 g)
(plus 2 tblsp. for top)

Cream the fat with the sugar and work in flour to make a stiff dough. (Use 4 oz. (125 g) sugar only). Mix in the fruit and nuts. Pat into a shallow, greased 12" × 8" tin and prick top with a fork. Sprinkle with the 2 tablespoons of Demerara sugar. Bake at 350°F/180°C/Gas Mark 4 for 30 minutes.

Frostow W.I.

GRANNIES CRUNCH

9 oz. margarine (250 g)   9 oz. P. flour (250 g)
4 ½ oz. sugar (125 g)   ½ oz. baking powder (10 g)
7 oz. desiccated coconut (200 g) 1 oz. drinking chocolate or cocoa
2 oz. golden syrup (50 g)

Mix well and press into a Swiss roll tin. Put into a medium oven or cook until firm and brown. Ice whilst still hot with ½ lb (225 g) icing sugar and 1 oz. (25 g) drinking chocolate. Cut into fingers when cold.

Underbarrow W.I.

HOLLY BARS

4 oz. P. flour (125 g)	1 teasp. baking powder
Pinch of salt	3 oz. margarine (75 g)
6 oz. brown sugar (175 g)	1 egg
2½ oz. porridge oats (60 g)	Small tin of condensed milk
3 oz. dates (75 g)	4 oz. sultanas & currants (125 g)

Mix flour, baking powder and salt. Cream margarine and sugar, mix in flour, milk and egg. Stir in porridge oats and fruit. Line Swiss roll tin with greaseproof paper. Spread mixture on this. Bake until golden brown, 325°F to 350°F/170°C/Gas Mark 3–4. When cool, cover with chocolate or icing. Cut into fingers.

Cliburn W.I.

JAM CAKE

10 oz. S.R. flour (275 g)	2 oz. margarine (50 g)
2 oz. lard (50 g)	

Rub above ingredients together until they are like fine breadcrumbs and add a pinch of salt, 4 oz. (125 g) fine sugar and a medium egg, beaten. Do not make this too soft, but if not able to roll easily, add a small quantity of milk. Divide the mixture into four, roll one portion, place it on a baking tray and spread with jam. Roll a second portion and lay this on the top, sealing the edges. Repeat the process with the remainder and bake in a hot oven, 400°F/200°C/Gas Mark 6 for 10 minutes. Can be iced or sprinkled with icing sugar. This is an ideal 'pastry' for mince pies or the base of tray bakes requiring short pastry.

Allithwaite W.I.

JERICHO CAKE

4 oz. margarine or butter (125 g)	2-4 oz. dates (or dates and raisins)
5 oz. S.R. flour (150 g)	(50–125 g)
6 oz. sugar (175 g)	2 oz. chopped walnuts (50 g)
1 egg	

Melt margarine or butter in a pan. Add sugar. Chop up dates and walnuts. Add to pan, plus flour and egg. Beat well. Spread in a lightly greased Swiss roll tin, 22½ × 32 cms. Bake for 30 minutes at 350°F/175°C. Mark into squares and cut. Leave to cool in tin. Do not overcook.

Kendal Romney W.I.

LEMON MERINGUE BARS

4 oz. butter (or margarine) (125 g) 2 teasp. grated lemon rind
½ cup sugar Pinch of salt
2 eggs (separated) Extra ½ cup sugar
1 cup S.R. flour 1 tablsp. lemon juice
1 oz. ground almonds (25 g)

Beat butter and sugar together until light and fluffy. Fold in egg yolk, sifted flour, almonds, lemon rind and salt. Spread into greased Swiss roll tin and bake in moderate oven (350°F/180°C/Gas Mark 4) for 10 minutes. Remove from oven, cool slightly. Beat egg whites until soft peaks form, add sugar gradually and beat until stiff. Fold in lemon juice. Spread over slightly cooled base and bake for further 25 minutes. Cool slightly before cutting into slices.

Urswick W.I.

LEMON SHORTCAKE

4 oz. butter (125 g) 4 oz. S.R. flour (125 g)
4 oz. caster sugar (125 g) 1 teasp. lemon juice
1 medium egg Lemon Curd
4 oz. P. flour (125 g)

Cream butter and sugar until soft and creamy. Add egg. Beat well. Add sieved flours and lemon juice. Make smooth paste. Divide into 2 portions. Roll each piece to fit greased tin. Spread one with lemon curd to within ½" of edge. Put other piece on top and press together. Prick with fork. Crimp edges together. Bake at 350°F/180°C/Gas Mark 4 for 30–35 minutes.

Kendal Castle W.I.

LIESL'S WHACKY CAKE

1½ cups of S.R. flour 5 oz. melted margarine (150 g)
3 tblsp. cocoa 1 cup tepid water
1 cup caster sugar 1 level teasp. bi-carb. Soda
½ teasp. vanilla essence 1 dessp. Vinegar

Sift together flour and cocoa. Dissolve bi-carbonate of soda in vinegar. Put all ingredients into a bowl and mix. Put mixture into an 8" × 12" tray. Bake at 350°F/Gas Mark 3.

TOPPING
6 oz. icing sugar (175 g) 2 dessp. cocoa
1 oz. melted margarine (25 g) 2 tblsp. water

Kendal Castle W.I

MALLOW DELIGHTS (UNCOOKED)

10 digestive biscuits (crushed)
10 glacé cherries (chopped)
Approx. ½ 14 oz tin (400 g)
  Nestlés Condensed Milk

1 oz. sultanas (25 g)
1 oz chopped nuts (25 g)
10 marshmallows (chopped)

Mix all ingredients to a sticky paste and roll into a Swiss roll shape in sugar onto a piece of greaseproof paper. Place in fridge to set. When hardened, coat one half with melted chocolate, replace in fridge. When set, coat remaining half with chocolate. Serve thinly sliced.

Windermere W.I.

MARGARET'S MARS BARS

2 Mars Bars
2 oz. margarine (50 g)

Rice Krispies
Chocolate (melted)

Gently melt Mars bars and margarine. Add Rice Krispies to desired consistency. Set in a greased tin. Melted chocolate on top.

Underbarrow W.I.

MARSHAMALLOW CRISPIES

4 oz. toffee (Highland is suitable) (125 g)
4 oz. margarine (125 g)
5 oz. Rice Crispies (150 g)

20 marshmallows

Melt together gently the margarine and toffee. Remove from heat and mix in marshmallows thoroughly. Add Rice Crispies and mix well. Spread in greased Swiss roll tin and leave to set before cutting into fingers.

Underbarrow W.I.

MATILDA CAKE (very quick and easy)

10 oz. S.R. flour (275 g)
4 oz. sugar (125 g)
6 oz. margarine (175 g)

2 dessp. golden syrup
2 oz. cherries (50 g)
4 oz. sultanas (125 g)

Melt margarine and syrup in a pan, add all dry ingredients, mix well. Press into tin approx. 12"×7", bake for 25 to 30 minutes at 350°F/180°C/Gas Mark 4.

Arnside Knott W.I.

MINCEMEAT FINGERS

6 oz. S.R. flour (175 g)	A little beaten egg
1 level teasp. ground cinnamon	1 oz. Demerara sugar (25 g)
4 oz. butter or margarine (125 g)	4 tblsp. mincemeat (approx)
3 oz. caster sugar (75 g)	

Sieve flour and cinnamon, rub in butter, add sugar and enough egg to bind. Knead lightly. Divide dough in two. Press one into 7" square tin, cover with mincemeat, press other on top. Sprinkle Demerara sugar on top. Bake at 350°F/180°C/Gas Mark 4 for 40 minutes or until brown. Cool and cut into fingers.

Cliburn W.I.

MOCHA SQUARES

6 oz. S.R. flour (175 g)	3 eggs
6 oz. caster sugar (175 g)	1 tblsp. Camp coffee
6 oz. soft margarine (175 g)	1½ teasp. baking powder

Grease and line oblong tin 12" × 9". Place ingredients in a large bowl and beat until well blended. Bake in oven 350°F/180°C/Gas Mark 4 for approximately 35 minutes.

ICING

3 oz. soft margarine (75 g)	1 oz. drinking chocolate (25 g)
6 oz. icing sugar (175 g)	Small chocolate buttons
1 tblsp. Camp coffee	(for decoration)

Beat icing ingredients until smooth. Spread over cooled cake. Mark with a fork and decorate with chocolate buttons.

Soulby W.I.

MOIST CHOCOLATE AND ORANGE SQUARES

6 oz. soft margarine (175 g)	1 oz. cocoa (25 g)
6 oz. caster sugar (175 g)	7 oz P. flour (200g)
6 oz. golden syrup (175 g)	½ level teasp. bicarb. soda
2 large eggs	(dissolved in ½ pint milk (150 ml))
2 oz. ground almonds (50 g)	Grated rind of large orange

Grease and line tin 12" × 9". Put all ingredients in large bowl and beat well until mixture is well blended. Turn into tin and bake for 1¼ to 1½ hours. Oven 300°F/150°C/Gas Mark 2. Leave to cool in tin.

ORANGE BUTTER CREAM

3 oz. soft margarine (75 g)	3 tblsp. orange juice
8 oz. icing sugar (225 g)	

Beat icing ingredients until smooth. Spread over cake and mark with fork. Cut into squares and decorate with orange jelly slices if desired.

Soulby W.I.

NON-COOKING TREAT

4 oz. desiccated coconut (125 g)   1 small tin Nestlés milk
4 oz. margarine (125 g)   1 pckt. Marie biscuits (crushed)

Mix all together and press into sandwich tin. Leave in fridge for 24 hours. Ice thinly with lemon glace icing. Cut into strips.

Bowness W.I.

NUT AND FRUIT SHORTBREAD

8 oz. P. flour (225 g)   1 oz. ground rice (25 g)
3 oz. castor sugar (75 g)   6 oz. butter (175 g)
1 oz glacé cherries (25 g)   1 oz. Angelica (25 g)
2 oz. blanched almonds (50 g)

Cream the butter and sugar and add the ground rice and sieved flour. Chop cherries, angelica and half the almonds and add to the mixture. Place in a square shaped tin and press the remainder of the almonds lightly on top. Temperature: 350°F/180°C/Gas Mark 4. Time 30–40 minutes.

Arnside W.I.

OATY CURRANT TRIANGLES

4½ oz. margarine (125 g)   4½ oz. P. flour (125 g)
4½ oz. sugar (125 g)   6oz. rolled oats (175 g)
3 oz. syrup (75 g)   6 oz. currants (175 g)
Good pinch bicarb. soda

Melt margarine, sugar and syrup over a low heat. Add to dry ingredients of flour, oats, currants and bicarbonate of soda. Mix well. Spread into greased 11" × 7" Swiss roll tin. Bake in moderate oven 375°F/190°C/Gas Mark 5 for 20 minutes. Should be golden brown and still soft to touch. When cool, cut into triangles and place on wire tray.

Heversham W.I.

PARADISE CAKE

Short crust pastry   1 tea cup sultanas
Raspberry jam   2 oz. cut glacé cherries (50 g)
4 oz. margarine (125 g)   2 tblsp. ground rice
4 oz. caster sugar (125 g)   2 tblsp. ground almonds
1 egg   1 teasp. vanilla essence

Line a greased Swiss roll tin with shortcrust pastry and spread with raspberry jam. Cream together margarine and caster sugar. Add egg and beat well. Mix sultanas, cherries, rice, almonds and vanilla essence. Add to creamed mixture and mix well. Spread over pastry. Bake at 375°F/190°C/ for 45 minutes. When cooked, dredge with caster sugar while still hot. Cut into fingers when cold. 1 oz. (25 g) chopped walnuts may be added to the above mixture.

Tebay W.I.

RICH FRUIT SLICES

8 oz. short crust pastry (225 g) 1 egg
4 oz. margarine (125 g) 3 oz. ground almonds (75 g)
4 oz. sugar (125 g) 3 oz. ground rice (75 g)
1 lb 4 oz of currants and sultanas (575 g)
2 tblsp. chopped walnuts 2 tblsp. chopped cherries

Preheat oven to 325°F. Line tin approximately 8" × 11" with pastry. Beat together margarine and sugar. Add rest of ingredients and put into pastry case. Bake until top is set and brown.

Kendal W.I. Market

STRABANE FINGERS

1 cup flour ½ cup sugar
1 cup cornflakes 1 teasp. baking powder
1 cup coconut 6 oz. margarine (175 G)

Mix all dry ingredients. Melt margarine, add and mix well. Press into Swiss roll tin. Bake for 30 minutes in a medium oven.

TOPPING
8 oz. icing sugar (225 g) 2 level teasp. cocoa

Mix icing sugar and 2 level teaspoons of cocoa with a little warm water and ice while still warm. Leave to cool before cutting.

Underbarrow W.I.

SYDNEY'S SPECIAL

1 cup S.R. flour ½ cup sugar
1 cup Rice Krispies 6 oz. margarine (175 g)
1 cup coconut Cooking chocolate

Mix dry ingredients together. Stir in melted margarine. Press into base-lined 12" × 8" Swiss roll tin. Cook at 350°F for about 25 minutes, or until golden brown. Cover with melted chocolate. Cut into squares whilst still warm.

Urswick W.I.

TEA-TIME FINGERS

4 oz. butter or margarine (125 g) ½ teasp. vanilla essence
5 oz. Demerara sugar (150 g) 4 oz. sultanas (125 g)
2 eggs 2 oz. choc. Dots (50 g)
6 oz. S.R. flour (175 g) (coarsely chopped)

Grease 11" × 7" tin. Cream butter and sugar. Add eggs, beat again. Stir in remaining ingredients, mix well. Put into tin, level top. Bake at 350°F/180°C/Gas Mark 4 for about 40 minutes. Leave until cold then cut into fingers. Makes 20 pieces.

Kendal Castle W.I.

WESTMORLAND CURRANT PASTY

1 lb of P. flour (450 g)
½ lb lard (225 g)
2 oz. butter (50 g)
Pinch of salt
A little sugar

1 lb currants in a pan with (450 g)
1 oz. butter (25 g)
4 oz. caster sugar (125 g)
1 oz. lemon peel (25 g)
1 teasp. of rum

Heat ingredients in pan and allow to cool. Mix flour, lard, salt, sugar and butter to a dough with water. Divide dough into two portions and line a Swiss roll tin with one portion. Cover with currant mixture and cover that with remaining pastry. Bake at 400°F.

Bampton W.I.

WESTMORLAND DREAM CAKE

4 oz. butter (125 g)
4 oz. P. flour (125 g)

1 oz. soft brown sugar (25 g)

Rub fat into dry ingredients. Place in a Swiss roll tin and flatten out. Bake for 20 minutes at 180°C/350°F. Allow to cool.

TOPPING

8 oz. soft brown sugar (225 g)
1 oz. P. flour (25 g)
Pinch of salt

½ teasp. baking powder
3 oz. coconut (75 g)
4 oz. chopped walnuts (125 g)

Mix all together. Add 2 beaten eggs. Mix well. Spread on top of cooked cake. Bake for 20 minutes at 180°C/350°F. Cut while warm. Allow to cool.

Scales W.I.

Gingerbreads

Almond Gingerbread
Coffee Gingerbread
Connoisseurs Parkin
Economical Gingerbread
Gingerbread Sponge
Grasmere Gingerbread
Honey Gingerbread
Microwave Gingerbread
Orange Gingerbread
Parkin
Rich Gingercake
Sticky Gingerbread

ALMOND GINGERBREAD

5 eggs
10 oz. sugar (275 g)
¼ oz. ground ginger (5 g)
Pinch of nutmeg
4 oz. candied peel, diced (125 g)

9 oz. flour (250 g)
6 oz. almonds, blanched (175 g)
¼ oz. bicarbonate of soda (5 g)
½ wine glass milk

Beat egg yolks and sugar until light; add nutmeg and ginger. Beat egg whites until stiff and add, together with peel. Stir in lightly, the previously warmed flour. Add 4 oz. (125 g) almonds, split into halves; finally add milk and bicarbonate of soda. Line baking tin with buttered paper. Pour in the mixture and brush top with milk, covering with remaining almonds, finely chopped.

Bake in moderate oven for 35 minutes; turn out and cut into squares.

Kendal Strickland W.I.

COFFEE GINGERBREAD

7 oz. S.R. flour (200 g)
4 oz. margarine (125 g)
2 oz. light brown soft sugar (50 g)
3 oz. syrup (75 g)

2 teasp. ground ginger
2 teasp. instant coffee
4 fluid oz. hot water (120 ml)
2 eggs

Dissolve the coffee in the hot water. Melt margarine, syrup and sugar and add to sieved dry ingredients. Mix in the beaten eggs and coffee mixture. Stir well. Pour into a greased and lined 8" square tin and bake at 180°C/350°F for 40–45 minutes.

Barbon W.I.

CONNOISSEUR'S PARKIN

9 oz. wholemeal flour (250 g)
6 oz. dark brown sugar (175 g)
4 oz. pin head oatmeal (125 g)
2-3 heaped teasps. ground ginger
1 egg
¼ pint milk (150 ml)

7 oz. black treacle (200 g)
3 oz. golden syrup (75 g)
1 rounded teasp. bicarb. of soda
1 dessp. vinegar
3 oz. soft margarine (75 g)
2 oz. lard (50 g)

Put flour, sugar, oatmeal, ginger and egg in a bowl and mix together. Put treacle, syrup and fats in a pan and melt carefully. Be careful that this mixture does not boil, otherwise you are in a lot of trouble! Add this mixture to the dry ingredients and mix well. Pour on the milk and mix. Now add the bicarbonate of soda and pour on the vinegar. Stir all well together. The mixture will now be easy to pour into a well-greased roasting tin. Bake at Gas Mark 4/350°F for one hour.

Arnside W.I.

ECONOMICAL GINGERBREAD

4 cups P. flour	2 tblsp. syrup
1½ cups sugar	2 tblsp. treacle
1 cup fat, melted or oil	2 teasp. ground ginger
1 cup warm milk	2 teasp. bicarb. of soda

Put flour, sugar and ground ginger into a bowl. Melt fat, syrup and treacle and add to dry ingredients. Warm milk and add bicarbonate of soda immediately to the mixture. Pour at once into a greased roasting tin and bake at 350°F for 1 hour approximately.

Burton W.I.

GINGERBREAD SPONGE

2 oz lard (50 g)	1 teasp. ground ginger
2 oz. butter or margarine (50 g)	½ teasp. cinnamon
2 oz. sugar (50 g)	½ breakfast cup milk
½ lb syrup or treacle (225 g) (or mixture)	1 teasp. bicarb. of soda
½ lb P. flour (225 g)	1 egg (beaten)

In pan, melt syrup, lard, butter and sugar. Mix flour, ginger, and cinnamon in large bowl and add melted syrup etc. Add beaten egg. Dissolve bicarbonate of soda in milk and add to above mixture, beating well.
Bake at 150°C/300°F for 1 hour.

Killington W.I.

GRASMERE GINGERBREAD

8 oz. flour (225 g)	½ dessp. ground ginger
4 oz. brown sugar (125 g)	½ teasp. bicarb. of soda
4 oz. butter or margarine (125 g)	½ teasp. cream of tartar
1 tblsp. syrup	Pinch of salt

Mix dry ingredients. Cream fat and sugar, add syrup and then dry ingredients. Put into a greased Yorkshire pudding tin evenly and press down with the back of a spoon. Cook in a slow oven and cut into squares before cold.

Langdale W.I.

HONEY GINGERBREAD

6 oz. P. flour (175 g)
4 oz. clear honey (125 g)
1 oz margarine (25 g)
1 oz. dark brown sugar (25 g)
2 level teasp. ground ginger
1½ level teasp. mixed spice

½ level teasp. bicarb. of soda
Pinch ground cloves
1 tblsp. black treacle
2 tblsp. milk
1 medium egg (beaten)

Grease well and line a 6" square tin. Set oven to 180°C/350°F/Gas Mark 4. Sift flour, ginger, mixed spices, cloves and bicarbonate of soda into a bowl. Put honey into a saucepan with margarine, sugar and treacle and melt over a low heat. After making a dip in the flour mixture use a fork to briskly stir in the honey etc. with the beaten egg and milk but do not beat. When smooth and no longer streaky, transfer to prepared tin and bake for 1 hour in oven centre. Stand in tin for 10 to 15 minutes. Keep at least one day before cutting.

The Lakes W.I. Market

MICROWAVE GINGERBREAD – 650 WATT

3 oz. margarine (75 g)
6 oz. black treacle (175 g)
2 oz. soft dark brown sugar (50 g)
4 fl. oz. milk (120ml)
½ teasp. bicarb. of soda

6 oz. S.R. flour (175 g)
1 teasp. ground ginger
Good pinch mixed spice
1 large egg (beaten)

Place margarine, treacle, sugar and milk in a bowl and heat in microwave full power 2 ½ minutes. Sprinkle in bicarb. of soda sift flour and spices together and add the milk mixture and egg to dry ingredients. Mix until smooth. Pour mixture into a greased 7" round deep dish. Cook for 9-10 minutes on 2/3 power or until cake comes away from side of dish. Cool on rack.

Cliburn W.I.

ORANGE GINGERBREAD

¼ lb margarine (125 g)
¼ lb soft brown sugar (125 g)
6 oz. strong P. flour (175 g)
1 egg (beaten)
¼ pt milk (150 ml)
Juice and finely grated rind of 1 orange
8" well greased tin.

3 oz. syrup (75 g)
3 oz treacle (75 g)
¼ teasp. salt
1 teasp. ground ginger
1 teasp. bicarb. of soda

Put flour, salt and ground ginger in large bowl. Mix egg, rind and orange juice into dry ingredients. In pan, slowly melt margarine, sugar, syrup and treacle then add milk and bicarbonate of soda. Mix all together (can use electric hand mixer). Pour into tin and bake at 120°C/240°F for 1 hour.

Pooley Bridge W.I.

PARKIN

8 oz. block margarine (225 g)
8 oz. Demerara sugar (225 g)
8 oz. black treacle (225 g)
  (golden syrup if preferred)
6 fl. oz. milk (180 ml)

12 oz S.R. wholemeal flour (350 g)
12 oz. medium oatmeal (350 g)
1 teasp. ginger
2 teasp. mixed spice
½ teasp. bicarb. of soda

Gently melt margarine, sugar and treacle in a large pan, add milk, stir well together. Mix flour with bicarbonate of soda and spices. Add oatmeal. Blend together, then add to the pan and mix well. An extra drop of milk may be required. Grease and flour a large roasting tin. Pour in the mixture and bake in a moderate oven (Gas Mark 4/350°F) until edges are firm. Cool a little before turning out. Improves with keeping for a few days.

Allithwaite W.I.

RICH GINGERBREAD

10 oz. S.R. flour (275 g)
1 level teasp. salt
2 level teasp. ginger
2 level teasp. cinnamon
½ level teasp. nutmeg

8 oz. Demerara sugar (225 g)
6 oz. hard margarine or veg. fat (175 g)
6 oz. golden syrup (175 g)
2 eggs
5 fl. oz. milk (150 ml)

3 oz. chopped raisins (75 g) & 3 oz. chopped walnuts are optional (75 g)

Grease oblong tin measuring about 9½" × 7½". Line bottom with greased paper. Sift all dry ingredients. Melt fat and syrup, allow to cool a little. Stir into dry ingredients with beaten eggs. Mix until smooth. Add milk and beat well. Turn into tin (mix will be like batter). Bake in moderate oven 325°F/Gas Mark 3 for 1 ½ hours. Cool in tin. Keeps well and freezes well.

Windermere W.I.

STICKY GINGERBREAD

8 oz. soft brown sugar (225 g)
4 oz. lard (125 g)
12 oz. P. flour (350 g)
½ pint milk (275 ml)

2 teasp. lemon juice
1½ level tblsp. ground ginger
1 level teasp. bicarb. of soda

Put sugar, lard, milk, lemon juice and ginger in a saucepan and stir until melted. Remove and beat for 10 minutes. Dissolve the soda in a little boiling water and mix well. Add the flour to make a stiff batter. Pour the mixture into a prepared 7" square tin. Bake in the oven at 180°C/350°F for about 1 hour until lightly brown.

Grayrigg W.I.

Small Cakes, Pastries Shortbreads etc

Almond Tarts
Brandy Snaps
Canadian Butter Tarts
Chocolate Ginger Balls
Coconut Castles
Coffee & Walnut Balls
Cornflour Nut Fingers
Cumbrian Rum Nicky
Eccles Cakes
Eclairs
Highland Shortbread
Meringues
Mincemeat Shortbread
Newton Rigg Mince Pies
Raspberry Buns
Scottish Shortbread
Shortbread
Shortbread with a Difference
Swiss Cakes
Swiss Rolls
Vanilla Slices
Viennese Fingers

ALMOND TARTS

6 oz. short crust pastry (175 g)   2 oz. semolina (50 g)
  (made with 1 egg yolk)   4 oz. ground almonds (125 g)
Raspberry jam   (or nut mix)
4 oz. granulated sugar (125 g)   1 egg
4 oz. icing sugar (125 g)   1 egg white (whipped)

Line tart tins with rolled out pastry cut into circles with pastry cutter. Mix dry ingredients together with 1 egg then fold in the whipped egg white. Put a spot of jam in each tart before filling with almond mixture. Bake 350°F.

Broughton Mills & Woodland W.I.

BRANDY SNAPS

2 oz. P. flour (50 g)   1 teasp. lemon juice
2 oz. butter (50 g)   3 tblsp. syrup
2 oz. soft brown sugar (50 g)   Grated rind of ½ lemon
1 teasp. ground ginger   Whipped cream for filling

Mix together flour, ginger and lemon rind. Melt butter, sugar and syrup together in a pan, then stir in the flour mixture and lemon juice. Line a baking tray with silicone paper and drop ½ teasp. of mixture, well apart on to the paper. Allow room for spreading. Bake at 375°F for 10 minutes. Remove brandy snaps from paper and roll each around the greased handle of a wooden spoon. Allow to cool. Repeat baking until mixture is all used. Pipe a rosette of whipped cream inside each end.

Rydal W.I.

CANADIAN BUTTER TARTS

Short crust pastry   2 oz. chopped walnuts (50 g)
  (for approx. 18 tarts)   2 oz. currants (50 g)
3 oz. syrup (75 g)   1 egg
2 oz. soft brown sugar (50 g)   ¼ teasp. vanilla essence
1¼ oz. butter (25 g)

Cook syrup and sugar gently in a pan for 5 minutes. Cool slightly. Add butter and melt. Beat the egg and add to the contents of the saucepan, beating continuously. Add the rest of the ingredients and mix well. Put into pastry cases and cook at 400°F for 10 minutes then down to 325°F for 20–25 minutes. (The filling will be brown).

Milnthorpe W.I.

CHOCOLATE GINGER BALLS

4 oz. dark chocolate (125 g)
2 oz. butter (or marg.) (50 g)
1 cup icing sugar
2 egg yolks

2 oz. preserved ginger (50 g)
1 teasp. rum (optional)
Chocolate strands or sprinkles

Melt chocolate over hot water (or in microwave). Cream butter and sugar until light and fluffy, add egg yolks. Gradually stir in melted chocolate, add chopped ginger and rum, beat until mixture is firm. Refrigerate for 1 hour. Form teasp. of mixture into balls. Roll in chocolate sprinkles. Refrigerate until ready to serve. Makes approximately 20.

Urswick W.I.

COCONUT CASTLES

8 oz. dessicated coconut (225 g)
6 oz. granulated sugar (175 g)
2 dessp. P. flour

Pinch of salt
1 egg
5 glacé cherries

Mix dry ingredients together. Beat egg and then mix in gradually with a fork. Shape into cones with an egg-cup (rinse in cold water each time before refilling). Place on baking sheet. Place ¼ glacé cherry on top of each one. Bake in moderate oven (350°F) for 10 minutes. Makes 18.

Underbarrow W.I.

COFFEE AND WALNUT BALLS

2 oz. margarine (50 g)
4 oz. icing sugar (125 g)
2 oz. chopped walnuts (50 g)

3 oz. desiccated coconut (75 g)
1 dessp. instant coffee powder
Melted chocolate

Cream margarine and icing sugar. Beat in instant coffee powder. Fold in walnuts and coconut. Form into walnut-sized balls and chill until firm. Dip balls into melted chocolate and place onto greaseproof paper. Serve in small paper cases.

Burneside W.I.

CORNFLOUR NUT FINGERS

8 oz. butter or margarine (225 g)
8 oz. caster sugar (225 g)
8 oz. P. flour (225 g)
8 oz. cornflour (225 g)
1 egg

4 oz. dark chocolate (125 g)
1 teasp. instant coffee
2 teasp. rum
2 oz. finely chopped walnuts (50 g)

Beat butter and sugar to a cream. Sieve in flour and cornflour. Add beaten egg and mix well. Pipe in three inch fingers onto non-stick baking tray. Bake at 180°C for 15 minutes. Melt chocolate. Add coffee and rum and stir until all coffee is dissolved. Sandwich the fingers with this mixture then dip about ½ inch of each end into it and then immediately into the chopped nuts.

Bowness W.I.

CUMBRIAN RUM NICKY

8 oz. rich short crust pastry (225 g) 1 tblsp. Demerara sugar
4 oz. chopped dates (125 g)   1 tblsp. dark rum
1 tblsp. water   2 oz. softened butter (50 g)
3 medium cooking apples (peeled and sliced)

Line 8" pie plate with half the pastry, put in sliced apples and scatter with sugar. Mix rum, water, butter and dates and spread over the apples. Top with remaining pastry, brush with milk. Bake at Gas Mark 6/400°F for 15 minutes and Gas Mark 4/350°F for a further 15 minutes until golden brown.

Burneside W.I.

ECCLES CAKES

8 oz. flaky pastry, well chilled (225 g) A little grated nutmeg
2 oz. butter (50 g)   or mixed spice
2 oz. soft brown sugar (50 g)   2 oz. cut mixed peel (50 g)
4 oz. currants (125 g)   A little milk or beaten egg
Caster sugar

Melt butter and stir in the sugar, add the fruit, peel and spice and mix together. Cool slightly. Roll out the pastry very thinly, cut into 6" rounds. Place a tablespoon of filling on each round, damp the pastry edges, draw to the centre covering the filling, and pinch well together. Turn smooth side up; flatten gently with the rolling pin so the currants just show through, keeping the cakes round. Make three small cuts on the top, brush with beaten egg or milk and dust with caster sugar. Place on baking sheet and bake at 425°F/210°C/Gas Mark 7 for about 15–20 minute until golden brown.

ECLAIRS

CHOUX PASTRY
4 oz P. flour (125 g)   ¼ pint water (150 ml)
2 oz. butter or margarine (50 g) 3 eggs (No. 4)

Place fat in water and melt over gentle heat, then bring to boil. Remove from heat and stir in flour until mixture forms a ball. Allow to cool. Add lightly beaten eggs gradually and mix thoroughly. Pipe mixture in size required, on a well greased tray which has been run under cold tap leaving a film of water on tray. Place in hot oven 220°C for approximately 20 minutes. Slit down side and leave to cool. Fill with whipped cream and coat with chocolate or coffee water icing.

Cliburn W.I.

HIGHLAND SHORTBREAD

6 oz. butter or margarine (175 g)   8 oz. P. flour (225 g)
4 oz. soft brown sugar (125 g)   ¼ teasp. salt

Mix all ingredients, knead well and roll into a sausage shape. Roll in Demerara sugar, wrap in greaseproof paper and refrigerate overnight. Cut into slices and bake at 325°F for 15–20 minutes or until golden.

Crosthwaite Lyth W.I.

MERINGUES

(36 from 1 egg white)
1 egg white   1 teasp. vinegar
6 oz. caster sugar (175 g)   2 teasp. baking powder
2 tblsp. boiling water   Whipped cream for filling
½ teasp. vanilla essence

(An electric mixer needed otherwise beating is quite hard work).

Flour a baking sheet. Combine unbeaten egg white with sugar and leave overnight.
Next day place in mixing bowl and whisk for 2 minutes at slow speed. Add boiling water, vanilla and vinegar and whisk at a medium-fast speed for 15 minutes (if using a hand whisk you would need to continue for at least another 10 minutes). Fold in baking powder. Fill a piping bag fitted with a star tube and pipe on prepared baking sheet. Put into a very cool oven (240°F/Gas Mark ½) for 1 hour, but after 20 minutes or so take a peep and if meringues are going a little brown, cover with foil or greaseproof paper. Turn off heat. Leave meringue in oven to cool. Sandwich together with cream.

Windermere W.I.

MINCEMEAT SHORTBREAD

6 oz. P. flour (175 g)   2 oz. caster sugar (50 g)
4 oz. butter or margarine (125 g)   4 tblsp. mincemeat

Cream butter and sugar together and work in the flour and mincemeat. Knead well and press mixture into an 8" round cake tin. Prick all over and bake at 325°F for 30–40 minutes. Sprinkle with caster sugar and cut into wedges.

Kendal Romney W.I.

NEWTON RIGG MINCE PIES

BASE PASTRY TOP PASTRY

8 oz. P. Flour (225 g)	3 oz. margarine (75 g)
2 oz. lard (50 g)	1 oz. sugar (25 g)
2 oz. margarine (50 g)	1 dessp. beaten egg
2 teasp. sugar (caster)	3 oz. P. flour (75 g)
2 tblsp. beaten egg	
Mincemeat for filling	Icing sugar for dredging

Make base pastry. Rub fat into flour, add sugar to egg. Add egg and sugar to fat and flour mixture. Knead gently. Make top pastry. Beat margarine and sugar to a dropping consistency. Add beaten egg and beat well. Add flour and mix well together. Place in piping bag with small meringue star pipe. Roll out pastry for base ⅛" thick and line patty tins. Fill well with mincemeat, and pipe top pastry round the edge. Bake for 10–15 minutes until golden brown. Gas Mark 6/400°F. When cool dredge lightly with icing sugar.

For special occasion a rosette of whipped cream may be piped in the centre.

Urswick W.I.

RASPBERRY BUNS

6 oz. S.R. flour (175 g)	1 small egg
3 oz. sugar (75 g)	Raspberry jam
3 oz. margarine (block) (75 g)	

Rub margarine into flour, add sugar then beaten egg to make a stiff paste. Roll into balls between the hands, makes about nine. Roll into sugar either soft brown or granulated. Place on greased baking tins. Make a hole in the centre with handle of wooden spoon, put a little jam in hole and then nip hole together. Bake at Gas Mark 5/375°F/190°C

Allithwaite W.I.

SCOTTISH SHORTBREAD

4 oz. sugar (125 g)	12 oz. P. flour (350 g)
8 oz. margarine (225 g)	1 tablsp. Farola or Semolina

Cream margarine and sugar. Add flour and Farola. Press into a sandwich tin and cook at 300°F for 1-1½ hours.

Holme W.I.

SHORTBREAD

½ lb P. flour (225 g)   5 oz. butter (150 g)
3 oz. caster sugar (75 g)   Split almonds

Beat the butter to a cream, add the sugar and beat in well. Add the flour gradually until all is absorbed. Then work up with the hands into balls; do not roll out but press into a well greased, flat tin until even all over, then place split almonds at intervals on top. Bake in moderate oven for about ½ hour. Heat about 300°F. The result should be a pale biscuit colour. Take from oven and mark into pieces of the size you like. Leave to cool.

Underbarrow W.I.

SHORTBREAD WITH A DIFFERENCE

3 oz. P. flour (75 g)   4 oz. butter (125 g)
2 oz. caster sugar (50 g)   Grated rind 1 orange
1 oz. ground almonds (25 g)   ½ oz. flaked almonds (10 g)
2 oz. cornflour (50 g)

Sift flour and cornflour together. Cream butter until soft. Add 2 oz. (50g) caster sugar and continue to beat until mixture is light and fluffy. Add orange rind. Work in flour mixture a tablespoon at a time. Stir in ground almonds. Place mixture on baking tin, allowing for a little spreading during cooking. Flatten mixture to form an 8" round. Flute edges, prick shortbread with a fork. Mark into 12 sections with the back of a knife. Sprinkle with flaked almonds and a little caster sugar. Chill for 15 minutes. Cook 335°F/Gas Mark 3 for 35 minutes until pale golden brown.

Windermere W.I.

SWISS CAKES

12 oz. butter (350 g)   1½ oz. custard powder (40 g)
3 oz. icing sugar (75 g)   1½ oz cornflour (40 g)
9 oz. P. flour (250 g)

Cream together butter and icing sugar until very soft. Gradually work in the flour, custard powder, cornflour and a few drops of vanilla essence until smooth. Pipe with ½" star nozzle into paper cases. Bake 180°F for about ½ hour. Dredge with icing sugar and put a dab of stiff jam in the centre.

Underbarrow W.I.

SWISS ROLL

3 eggs   4½ oz. S.R. flour (125 g)
4 oz. caster sugar (125 g)

Warm bowl slightly. Place eggs and sugar in bowl and whisk until thick, white and fluffy. Sift half the flour over the surface and fold in gently using a balloon whisk. Sift the rest of the flour over the mixture and fold in again and whisk. Spread the mixture quickly into a large, greased and lined Swiss roll tin. Bake at 425°F/210°C/Gas Mark 7 for about 8 minutes. Turn out onto greaseproof paper sprinkled with caster sugar, trim short end of Swiss roll, then spread with warm jam. Roll carefully, when cold, trim the ends to leave a straight edge with jam showing. If filling with cream roll up the cake and sugared paper together whilst hot, when cold carefully unroll and fill with jam and cream, then trim ends.

Cliburn W.I.

VANILLA SLICES

12 oz. puff pastry (350 g)

Roll pastry out thinly and cut into equal sized slices. Bake at 425°F/210°C/Gas Mark 7.

CONFECTIONERS CUSTARD (CRÉME PATISSIERE)
3 egg yolks   1 oz. flour (25 g)
½pint milk (275 ml)   4 oz. caster sugar (125 g)
1 vanilla pod (or few drops vanilla essence)

Place the flour, sugar and egg yolks in a bowl. Place milk and vanilla pod in a thick pan over a low heat and allow to come to just before boiling point *slowly*. Half fill the under pan of a double saucepan with water. Place over a low heat so that the water comes to a slow simmer. Whisk egg yolk mixture to a light foamy batter. Pour on heated milk and whisk again, ending with a good stir with a wooden spoon; make sure it is well mixed in. Turn mixture into the top of the double saucepan, raise heat slightly just enough for steam to filter through and then stir steadily until mixture coats back of a wooden spoon thickly. Allow to cool before filling the vanilla slices. Coat with glacé icing.

Cliburn W.I.

VIENNESE FINGERS

4 oz. S.R. flour (125 g)   2 oz. icing or caster sugar (50 g)
4 oz. P. flour (125 g)   ½ teasp. of vanilla essence
7 oz. margarine (200 g)

Cream fat, sugar and vanilla. Add flour gradually. Put in icing bag with large rose nozzle then pipe into fingers or rosettes. Cook in oven 375°F/Gas Mark 5 for approximately 20 minutes. When cool sandwich together with butter icing and dip into melted chocolate, at one end.

Clifton W.I.

Gluten-Free Recipes

Do you recognise this symbol? No? Well, this is the symbol that indicates to the coeliac sufferers amongst us that a particular food will not upset our digestive system, because it contains no gluten. This means to the everyday cook that we must not use any ingredients containing wheat, rye, barley or oats when cooking food for our friends who cannot tolerate gluten.

Cooking for a gluten-free diet need not be difficult because there are many popular dishes that are already gluten-free. Examples are omelettes, risotto, sauces thickened with cornflour, meringues, chocolate Rice Krispies – the list is quite lengthy.

Here are just a few recipes that you may like to try.

Almond Fingers
Cheesecake Base
Chocolate & Hazelnut Cookies
Coconut Pyramids
Light Sponge Cake
Macaroons
Rice Flour Balls
Rice Flour Sponge Cake
Rice Flour Sponge Cake
- Christmas Log
Rice Flour Sponge Cake
- Truffle Triangle

ALMOND FINGERS

Makes 24

100 g cornflour · 1 tblsp. sherry
50 g caster sugar · 1 teasp. egg yolk
50 g butter

TOPPING
1 egg white · 25 g chopped blanched almonds
25 g caster sugar

Mix cornflour and caster sugar in a bowl, work in the butter by rubbing and kneeding. Combine sherry and egg yolk and use to bind the mixture to a soft dough. Roll out to 3mm thick and cut into fingers. Beat egg whites until stiff, then beat in sugar. Spread this on the biscuits like an icing and sprinkle chopped almonds on top. Bake slowly at 170°C for 30–40 minutes or until the biscuits are crisp and the topping firm and just coloured.
CAUTION – The biscuits must be rolled thinly or they will not cook in the same time as the topping.

Selside W.I.

CHEESECAKE BASE

75 g cornflakes – crushed · 50 g very soft brown butter or
25 g icing sugar – sifted · or margarine

Mix well and press flat into a 20 cm diameter loose-bottom tin.

Selside W.I.

CHOCOLATE & HAZELNUT COOKIES

Makes 15

2 egg whites · 50 g plain chocolate – grated
50 g caster sugar · 50 g ground or minced hazelnuts
50 g ground rice · 15 whole hazelnuts

Beat egg whites until stiff and gradually beat in sugar. Mix in ground rice, grated chocolate and ground hazelnuts. Put small heaps of the mixture on well-oiled baking trays or rice paper and place a whole nut on each. Bake at 190°C for 20–25 minutes or until firm.

Selside W.I.

COCONUT PYRAMIDS

8 oz. desiccated coconut (225 g) · 1 egg
6 oz. caster sugar (175 g)

Set oven to 130–150°C. Mix the dry ingredients and add beaten egg to form a crumbly consistency. Rinse a small egg-cup with cold water and lightly fill with mixture. Tap out onto an ungreased tin or rice paper. Rinse the egg-cup after each pyramid. Bake for 15–20 minutes or until just set and brown on top.

Lupton W.I.

LIGHT SPONGE CAKE

(also suitable for Swiss roll and flan base)

3 large eggs	½ oz. cornflour (10 g)
1 oz. potato flour* (25 g)	3 oz. caster sugar (75 g)
1 oz. banana flour* (25 g)	2 tblsp. cold water
1 oz. ground hazelnuts (25 g)	

*Available from Health Food Shops

Grease 8" × 1½" sandwich tin and line base. Separate egg yolks. Whisk egg whites until stiff, add 2 oz. (50 g)of caster sugar and whisk again. Whisk egg yolks until thick, add 1 oz. (25 g) caster sugar, whisk, add one tablespoon cold water, whisk, add another tablespoon cold water and whisk again. Fold this yolk mixture into egg whites with a metal spoon, and then fold in sieved flour and ground hazelnuts. Pour into sandwich tin and bake on middle shelf (top shelf if using Swiss roll tin). Bake at Gas Mark 5/190°C/375°F for 40 minutes or until the top is springy to the touch. Allow the cake to shrink slightly before turning out on wire tray and removing lining paper. When cold, split carefully and fill with preserve or fresh fruit and whipped cream.

Windermere W.I.

MACAROONS

2 oz. ground almonds (50 g)	A few drops vanilla or
3 oz. caster sugar (75 g)	almond essence
1 teasp. ground rice	A few flaked almonds
White of one egg	

Set oven 130–150°C. Place a sheet of rice paper on a baking sheet. Mix dry ingredients. Add essence and slightly beat white of egg to make a stiff paste. Beat well. Place teasp. of mixture on rice paper and flatten slightly. Place a piece of flaked almond on each. Bake for 20–25 minutes until pale brown.

VARIATION
Chocolate Macaroons

Add ¼ oz. (10 g) grated chocolate or ¼ oz. (5 g) cocoa to dry ingredients.

Lupton W.I.

RICE FLOUR BALLS

4 oz. margarine or butter (125 g)	8 oz. rice flour (225 g)
6 oz. soft brown sugar (175 g)	½ teasp. bicarb. of soda
½ egg	1 teasp. cream of tartar
2 teasp. ground ginger	

Set oven at 160°C. Grease baking sheets. Cream margarine and sugar. Beat in ½ egg. Sieve dry ingredients together. Fold dry ingredients into creamed mixture. Take walnut-sized pieces and roll into balls. Place on greased baking tray and flatten slightly. Bake for 15–20 minutes. Leave on the tray to cool slightly before removing.

Lupton W.I.

RICE FLOUR SPONGE CAKE

2 eggs   2 oz. rice flour (50 g)
2 oz. caster sugar (50 g)

Set oven at 150°C. Grease and base-line a sandwich cake tin. Whisk the eggs and sugar together until very stiff and creamy – like whipped cream. Very carefully sieve rice flour over egg mixture. Quickly and very lightly, fold in the rice flour using a *metal* spoon. Pour into prepared tin. Bake for 30 minutes.

This sponge cake may be used for a sponge flan and for a trifle base.

Lupton W.I.

RICE FLOUR SPONGE CAKE – CHRISTMAS LOG

1½ lb rice flour sponge cake (700 g)   2 oz. carob powder (or
4 oz. mincemeat or apricot jam (125 g)   cocoa) (50 g)
2 oz. shelled walnuts – chopped (50 g)   3-4 tblsp. orange juice,
                                             sherry or rum

Crumble the cake. Add mincemeat or apricot jam, walnuts and carob powder. Add sufficient liquid to give a moist consistency and work together until smooth. Turn onto a working surface and work into a log shape before putting into a cool place. Sprinkle with icing sugar when set.

Lupton W.I.

RICE FLOUR SPONGE CAKE – TRUFFLE TRIANGLE

1½ lb rice flour sponge cake (700 g)   Orange juice and/or sherry/
4 oz. mincemeat or apricot jam (125 g)   rum to mix (3-4 tblsp.)
2 oz. shelled walnuts – chopped (50 g)   Toasted flaked almonds
2 oz. carob powder (or cocoa) (50 g)   to decorate
Glacé icing to cover

Crumble the cake into a basin. Add mincemeat, apricot jam, walnuts and carob powder. Add sufficient liquid to give a moist but firm consistency. Work the mixture together until fairly smooth. Turn the mixture onto a working surface and press into a triangular shape. Place the cake on the cake wire. Cover with chocolate or vanilla icing. Sprinkle with flaked almonds and leave to set. Serve cut into slices.

Lupton W.I.

Savoury Sandwich Fillings

Apple and Date
Apple and Raisin
Asparagus Rolls
Aubergine with Egg
Beetroot and Egg
Carrot and Marmite
Celery, Cucumber, Tomato and Onion
Cream Cheese, Honey and Nuts
Date and 'Philly'
Egg and Chutney
Kipper Spread
'Mock Crab'
Potted Meat
Potted Salmon
Shrimp, Celery, Cheese and Strawberry
Smoked Salmon Paté
Stack Sandwiches
Tomato and Cheese Spread
Tuna and Cream Cheese
Tuna and Curry
Tuna Paté
Waldorf Spread

APPLE AND DATE

Peel and core one large eating apple. Put this, and approximately four dried dates through mincer. Mix and moisten with juice of half a lemon.

Underbarrow W.I.

APPLE AND RAISIN

Peel and core an eating apple. Slice finely. Use a layer of sliced apple and a layer of dried raisins.

Underbarrow W.I.

ASPARAGUS ROLLS

Remove crusts from thinly cut brown bread; butter and roll round an asparagus tip.

Crook W.I.

AUBERGINE WITH EGG

1 aubergine	2 tblsp. oil
1 small onion	vinegar and salt
2 hard-boiled eggs	

Cut the aubergine into thin slices without peeling. Fry in the oil with the onion until lightly browned. Put this mixture, together with the eggs, through a mincer until fine. Season to taste, with vinegar and salt.

Underbarrow W.I.

BEETROOT AND EGG

Spread slice of bread with scrambled egg; cover with cooked beetroot (NOT in vinegar) and cover again with a slice of buttered bread.

Underbarrow W.I.

CARROT AND MARMITE

Spread a slice of bread with a little Marmite, and add finely grated raw carrot. Cover with slice of buttered bread.

Underbarrow W.I.

CELERY, CUCUMBER, TOMATO AND ONION

Finely chop and mix together the above ingredients; add grated cheese and enough mayonnaise to allow mixture to spread easily.

Pooley Bridge and District W.I.

CREAM CHEESE, HONEY AND NUTS

3 oz. cream cheese (75 g)   1 oz. toasted chopped nuts (25 g)
1 level teasp. thin honey   A little grated orange rind

Mix all the ingredients together and spread on wholemeal bread. It is very good as an open sandwich.

Kendal Castle W.I.

DATE AND 'PHILLY'

'Philadelphia' cream cheese. Cooking dates, finely chopped. Spread one slice of brown bread thickly with cream cheese and sprinkle with the chopped dates. Cover with a buttered slice of bread.

Dufton W.I.

EGG AND CHUTNEY

Crush yolks of three hard-boiled eggs and add chutney gradually to form a moist paste. Spread this on slice of buttered bread. Shred whites of eggs and place on top of yolk mixture. Cover with second slice of bread. Press together and trim.

Lowther W.I.

KIPPER SPREAD

(Smoked salmon and smoked trout can be used instead of kipper)
8 oz. cream cheese (225 g)   4 oz. cooked, flaked kipper (125 g)
4 tblsp. single cream   free of skin and bone
1 tblsp. lemon juice   Salt, pepper and Tabasco to taste
1 spring onion
1 sprig parsley (both finely chopped)

Mix all ingredients together to make a paste. (The flakes of the fish should be visible).

Preston Patrick & Preston Richard W.I.

MOCK CRAB

¼ lb tomatoes skinned (125 g)   1 oz. grated hard cheese (25 g)
  or small tin of tomatoes   1 small egg
1 tblsp. breadcrumbs   Seasoning
1 oz. butter (25 g)

Beat tomatoes to a pulp. Add crumbs and butter. Cook slowly in saucepan for a few minutes. Add grated cheese, beaten egg and seasoning. Stir until it thickens. (Can be potted and will keep for a day or two in fridge).

Windermere W.I.

POTTED MEAT

2 lb lean beef (900 g)　　　　½ pint cold water (275 ml)
3 oz. butter (75 g)　　　　　A little anchovy sauce
2 cloves

Cut the beef into small pieces, place in a stew pot with the water and cloves. Cover tightly and allow to simmer gently until meat is tender. When cool, pass through a mincer, (or food processor) season with salt and pepper, mix well with the butter (melted) and add some of the gravy from the meat. Press into small pots and cover with melted butter. Allow to set before using.

Bowness-on-Windermere W.I.

POTTED SALMON

Remove skin and bones from salmon. (Can be tinned or freshly cooked). Pound the salmon in a mortar with the butter, a little anchovy sauce, a little lemon juice and salt, pepper and cayenne. (Alternately mix in a food processor). When thoroughly mixed, put into small jars or ramekins and cover with melted butter. Can be kept for a little while in fridge, before using. When using, spread one side of a buttered slice of bread with the salmon mixture; cut some cucumber very thinly and place over salmon mixture; cover with another slice of bread.

Crook W.I.

SHRIMP, CELERY, CHEESE AND STRAWBERRY

4 oz. shrimps, finely chopped (125 g)　　8 large strawberries
2 ribs celery finely diced　　　　　　　finely sliced
8 oz. cream cheese (225 g)　　　　　16 slices white bread
　(beaten with salt and pepper)

Mix together the first three items with fork. Lightly butter the bread. Layer the strawberries over 8 slices of bread and then spread with the filling and cover with remaining 8 slices of bread.

Cliburn W.I.

SMOKED SALMON PATÉ

4 oz. smoked salmon pieces (125 g)　　1 tblsp. lemon juice
2 oz. melted butter (50 g)　　　　　A little salt and
2 oz. cream cheese (50 g)　　　　　ground black pepper

Put the salmon, cream cheese, lemon juice and half the butter into a blender (or processor) and mix until smooth. Season to taste and put in a small pot. Pour over the remaining butter and leave in a cool place to set.

Underbarrow W.I.

STACK SANDWICHES

Softened butter for spreading. 8 large slices white bread. 8 large slices brown bread.

FILLINGS
4 oz. duck paté (125 g)
3 hard boiled eggs chopped and mixed with mustard and cress, mayonnaise, salt and black pepper.
4 oz. (125 g) cream cheese and 4 oz. (125 g) dates chopped into small pieces.

Spread 4 slices of buttered BROWN bread evenly with paté and cover each with a slice of WHITE bread, butter side down. Spread the top with butter.
Spread the egg mixture evenly over the top of each sandwich, then place a BROWN slice on top, butter side down. Spread the top with butter.
Spread the cream cheese over the sandwich stack and scatter the dates onto the cream cheese. Place remaining WHITE bread on top, buttered side down.

Wrap in cling film and chill until required. Then cut the crusts off, cut into 4 slices and halve each slice.

Dufton W.I.

TOMATO AND CHEESE SPREAD

8 oz. cream cheese (225 g)   Pinch of salt
1 medium sized ripe tomato   ½ teasp. paprika pepper
1 thin slice onion

Place all ingredients in a liquidiser or food processor, and blend until smooth.

Underbarrow W.I.

TUNA AND CREAM CHEESE

Mix equal amounts of tuna (or tinned salmon) and low fat cream cheese. Moisten with a little thick yoghurt. Beat until smooth then season to taste. Spread between slices of bread and butter. Put a little chopped watercress on top, before putting on the other slice.

Windermere W.I.

TUNA AND CURRY

Beat a tin of tuna with a little butter and add a good half teasp. curry. Spread between slices of bread.

Windermere W.I.

TUNA PATÉ

7 oz. tin tuna in oil (200 g)   1 tblsp. salad cream
1 large slice brown bread   Salt, pepper and vinegar to taste

Drain some of the oil from the fish, and trim the crusts from the bread. Put those in a liquidiser with the salad cream and process until paste forms. Season to taste. Alternatively, flake the fish with a fork and beat with the other ingredients. Season to taste. This can be used for sandwiches, or as a toast topping for winter teas.

Allithwaite W.I.

WALDORF SPREAD

100 g cottage cheese or   ½ Granny Smith apple (peeled
  light cream/full cream cheese   if preferred)
8" celery sticks, preferably   12 walnut halves
  the green end

Chop celery and walnuts very finely. Chop apple finely and sprinkle with lemon juice. Fold celery, nuts and apple into cheese.

Dentdale W.I.

NOTES

NOTES

NOTES

NOTES

Tea Time!